Vital Witnesses

Using Primary Sources in History and Social Studies

Mark Newman

ROWMAN & LITTLEFIELD
Lanham • Boulder • New York • London

Published by Rowman & Littlefield
A wholly owned subsidiary of The Rowman & Littlefield Publishing Group, Inc.
4501 Forbes Boulevard, Suite 200, Lanham, Maryland 20706
www.rowman.com

16 Carlisle Street, London W1D 3BT, United Kingdom

British Library Cataloguing in Publication Information Available

Library of Congress Cataloging-in-Publication Data

Newman, Mark, 1948–
  Vital witnesses : using primary sources in history and social studies / Mark Newman.
    pages cm
  Includes bibliographical references.
  ISBN 978-1-4758-1053-0 (pbk. : alk. paper) — ISBN 978-1-4758-1054-7 (electronic)
  1. History—Study and teaching (Middle school)—United States. 2. History—Study and
  teaching (Secondary)—United States. 3. Social sciences—Study and teaching (Middle
  school)—United States. 4. Social sciences—Study and teaching (Secondary)—United
  States. 5. History—Sources. 6. Social sciences—Sources. 7. Teaching—United
  States—Aids and devices. I. Title.
  D16.3.N45 2014
  907.1'273—dc23

                                                                              2014027477

∞™ The paper used in this publication meets the minimum requirements of American
National Standard for Information Sciences—Permanence of Paper for Printed Library
Materials, ANSI/NISO Z39.48-1992.

Printed in the United States of America

Contents

Preface   vii

Introduction: What Are Primary Sources?   xi

PART ONE: UNDERSTANDING PRIMARY SOURCES   1

The World of Primary Sources   1

Print Documents: Paper and Electronic   3

Visual Documents   6

Maps   8

Photographs   11

Editorial Cartoons   12

Film/Video   14

Fine Arts   17

Folk Culture and Mythology   20

The Built Environment   26

Material Culture   29

The Natural Environment   32

**PART TWO: HOW CAN PRIMARY SOURCES BE USED
IN THE CLASSROOM?**   37

The Big-Picture Inquiry-Based Learning Method   40

Classroom Exercises   44

Which Way Is Up?   46

What Did the Declaration of Independence Say?   52

European Immigrants Arriving in the United States, Early 1900s 55

What Type of Community Is It?   57

Using Primary Sources to Open a Unit of Study   60

*What Did Ancient Egyptian Society Need to Have to Build
the Pyramids?*   61

"I'd Rather Not Be on Relief"   63

*What Did a Community Need to Build and Maintain
This Structure?*   65

Document-Based Questions (DBQ)   66

Using Visuals to Meet the Needs of All Learners   70

PART THREE: ACCOMMODATING COMMON CORE   75

Accommodating Common Core Literacy Standards   75

Accommodating the C3 Framework   80

Bibliography   85

Preface

Vital Witnesses: Using Primary Sources in History and Social Studies is a successor to an earlier volume titled *Tuning In: Primary Sources in the Teaching of History*. Written by my colleague, Professor Gerald Danzer, and myself, *Tuning In* provided teachers with a guide on the theory and practice of primary source documents in secondary school history classes. Apparently, the volume filled a void, as *Tuning In* found its way into classrooms across the United States. *Vital Witnesses* seeks to perform a similar function, although in very different times.

Since *Tuning In* appeared in 1991, seismic changes have occurred in education, creating a need for a new volume on primary sources in history and social studies that accommodates these alterations. First, an array of millions of primary sources are readily available on the Internet on institutional sites such as the Library of Congress, the National Archives, and on more informal sites like YouTube.

Second, technological advances have enhanced our ability to create and to manipulate a variety of media. Common in the past, such manipulation is more pervasive today because almost anyone can alter a photograph or video by changing the colors, adding or eliminating people, or altering the position of items. Because it is so easy to post materials on the Internet, the source document and the site can raise trust issues.

Third, the dominance of assessment and standards has enhanced the status of primary sources. The document-based question (DBQ) is a basic component of Advanced Placement exams and a regular evaluation in many grades six through twelve social studies and history courses. Common Core literacy standards and the C3 Framework for State Social Studies Standards also have propelled primary sources to the forefront. They are all about the use of texts.

Most important, teachers know that using primary sources just makes sense. Primary sources engage students, bringing them closer to the people, places, and events being studied. Students learn the content by practicing reading, thinking, and communication skills.

For all of these reasons, the time is ripe for a new book on primary sources in history and social studies. *Vital Witnesses* seeks to fill a growing need among K–12 teachers for greater knowledge of primary sources and expanded strategies on using them effectively in the classroom. As the name suggests, it extends across both social studies and history, spanning grades K–12. It also can be used at the collegiate level, especially in teacher education courses.

The introduction, What Are Primary Sources?, opens the discussion. It places primary sources into context. They are defined and the difference between a primary and secondary source is explained. The subjective, incomplete nature of these vital witnesses is discussed, noting that their slippery nature is what makes them such valuable classroom resources. The impact of the digital age on primary sources is examined. In addition, a basic inquiry model for use in the classroom is provided.

Part 1, Understanding Primary Sources, explores the various types. Background information on the specific type is provided. The nature of each type is discussed. In some cases, modes of inquiry are included. The discussion of each kind of primary source includes a brief narrative and a chart.

Part 2, How Can Primary Sources Be Used in the Classroom?, examines the use of primary sources in the teaching and learning of history and social studies, stressing classroom-tested strategies and exercises. The innovative "big picture" inquiry-based learning model that provides an instructional framework is explained. Designed to meet differing classroom scenarios, a variety of exercises are provided. Document-based questions (DBQ) are discussed.

Also included is an all-learners curriculum to help teachers meet the needs of all students. The all-learner curriculum seeks to accommodate the related movements of differentiation and universal design for learning to meet the individual needs of students. It offers a strategy to help second-language learners and students with special needs to better use primary sources as learning texts. It also can be used for differentiation.

Part 3, Accommodating Common Core, describes these related reform movements. The goals of these efforts are identified.

Equally important, Common Core and the C3 Framework are examined to identify what they are and what they are trying to do versus what they are not and what they are not doing. Both focus primarily on skills, and each expressly states that they are not providing an entire curriculum, nor are they mandating how teachers should teach. Whether or not these caveats are followed in practice remains to be seen. A strategy is presented for accommodating both the Common Core standards and the C3 Framework that fits within any inquiry model.

Vital Witnesses closes with a select bibliography.

As is true of any book, but especially applying to this volume, thanks are due to numerous people for their support. First and foremost, this book would not have been possible without Professor Jerry Danzer. He has been a mentor, colleague, and friend for over twenty years. He enthusiastically supported the writing of *Vital Witnesses*. Many thanks to him for all he has done for me.

For the last ten years, I have directed a Library of Congress Teaching with Primary Sources (TPS) project under the auspices of the Federation of Independent Illinois Colleges and Universities. That experience has vastly improved my knowledge of primary sources and my ability to use primary sources to improve student learning.

In addition to the opportunity to delve deeply into primary source–based inquiry, TPS allowed me to meet and collaborate with an extraordinary team of university faculty and K–12 teachers. All deserve thanks, but especially Don Fouts, who recruited me for the project, and Professor Costas Spirou, who was assistant director for many years. The same collegiality has existed in my relations with the national TPS project staff and other project directors. My thanks go out to Vivian Awumey, the coordinator of TPS, who has strongly supported our efforts.

Thanks also are due to Tom Koerner, vice president and publisher at Rowman & Littlefield, for supporting *Vital Witnesses*, and Caitlin Crawford, assistant editor, who has provided much help with the book. I would be remiss not to thank Professor Jack Zevin, who is my collaborator on another project and provided the contact with Rowman & Littlefield.

Lastly and most importantly, thanks to my family for their support. My wife, Kim, has lived through the writing of *Vital Witnesses* and so many other projects. I thank her for her patience, her love, and her support.

Introduction

What Are Primary Sources?

Simply put, primary sources are the "stuff" of history and social studies. They make the scholarly study of history possible and perform a similar function in education. They are repositories of information, serving as potential archives that can be tapped to increase content knowledge. To fulfill their function, teachers and students must understand what primary sources are. They need to be aware of their nature. They also have to be able to open a dialogue with them, meaning the primary sources act as channels of communication. Opening those communication channels require students to develop literacy and critical-thinking skills so they can read the sources and make sense of them. Using primary sources as texts in the classroom integrates learning content with the building of skills.

Since scholars, teachers, and students also use textbooks, monographs, journal articles, and other works that seek to explain a topic or subject, answering the question, "What are primary sources?" poses problems for many teachers and students.

The unique quality of primary sources has often made them difficult to define. On its website, the Library of Congress offers this definition:

> Primary sources are the raw materials of history—original documents and objects which were created at the time under study. They are different from secondary sources, accounts or interpretations of events created by someone without firsthand experience.

Primary sources are firsthand, direct evidence. The key words are *firsthand* and *direct*. They imply being there, having a direct connection to a person, event, or place. But being there can have varied meanings. A participant's account of a battle is a primary source. It is firsthand, direct evidence by someone who was there at the time and place. An account of that battle by a person not at the scene but living at the same time may also be a primary source. It is firsthand, direct evidence of how people at the time viewed the battle from afar. An account by someone at a later time and/or place also can be a primary source. It reflects firsthand, direct evidence of the perspective from that future time and place.

So context helps define a primary source, as this brief example shows. In 1933 to 1934, Chicago celebrated its centennial by hosting the Century of Progress World's Fair. As part of the Fair, a map was created that showed the city of Chicago in 1833. Is this map a primary source? The quick answer is "no," because the map was created one hundred years after the city it seeks to show. And if we are looking for a map made in 1833 to show Chicago at that time, "no" is correct. But if we evaluate the map as a later depiction, than the answer is "yes." It is a primary source of how people in 1933 perceived what Chicago looked like a century earlier.

Similarly, *firsthand* and *direct* relate to the topic of study. The history textbook is seldom considered a primary source. But if the topic of study is how U.S. history textbooks have covered the Civil War, those textbooks are firsthand, direct evidence of that coverage.

The flip side concerns what is not a primary source. As the above definition indicates, a key factor is whether the creator has firsthand experience. To assess a source's status, see if it fits the time, place, and topic criteria of being firsthand and direct. If it does not fit those criteria, then it is a secondary source.

In general, secondary sources tend to be works that use primary sources to analyze or evaluate topics or phenomena. They tell the story one or more steps removed from the person, time, or place. Books or journal articles written by historians and textbooks are examples of secondary sources. Some scholars go one step further and identify tertiary sources, citing the encyclopedia as examples.

The caveat, as the discussion here shows, is that shifting context can affect whether a source is primary or not.

WHY ARE PRIMARY SOURCES
VALUABLE CLASSROOM RESOURCES?

A primary source is a document that provides information. When we look into the derivation of the word *document*, an intriguing fact emerges. The Online Etymology Dictionary states that *document* is derived from the Latin *docere*, meaning "teach."

A document teaches. How effectively a primary source teaches depends upon how it is used in the classroom. The goal is to make students responsible for their learning so that they increase their mastery of content by developing important literacy, problem solving, and possibly cooperative work skills.

Three important steps to reach the goal of student responsibility and to allow primary sources to reach their full potential as documents are:

1. Understanding the nature of primary sources and exploiting that nature to promote student learning.
2. Recognizing that primary sources can place students into the time and place being studied, bringing them closer to the topic and people.
3. Situating the study of primary sources within a larger inquiry model so that the sources are integrated into the flow of learning.

Understanding the nature of primary source documents is essential. Each primary source document has a specific story to tell from a certain perspective influenced by the attitudes and beliefs of its creator, the type of primary source it is, and possibly the subject of the source. As readers, we bring our own perspective to the study of the source. In addition, the story is limited by that perspective and how much information the document can present.

As a result, by nature, primary sources are subjective and incomplete. Because it presents a particular viewpoint, a primary source is not neutral. Nor is it objective or necessarily accurate. As a single text, it can only relate part of the story. What teachers and students need to realize is that the subjective, incomplete nature of primary sources makes them slippery documents, but they are vital witnesses and learning resources if approached correctly.

When teachers understand the nature of primary sources, they can use that understanding to promote student learning. Simply put, primary source–based learning makes students think. The subjective, incomplete nature of primary sources means that students need to approach them with a healthy dose of skepticism. An overarching question seeking an answer throughout the analysis of a primary source is: Why should I believe what the source says?

In many instances, the first task is evaluating the source to ensure it is authentic, that it actually is what it claims to be. Historians call this task establishing the provenance, meaning the source is the original version created at the appropriate time and place. Establishing provenance begins by identifying the title, author, and any other information that describes the creation of the document to place it in the appropriate people, time, and place context.

Recall the 1933 map of Chicago. Checking its provenance for context would eliminate it as a contemporary document that depicted the city at its beginning, but not as a reflection of ideas a century later. In a sense, evaluating authenticity

Introduction

has students act as historical CSI (Crime Scene Investigation) agents conducting a forensic investigation on the source.

The next task is mining the source for content. Despite their slipperiness, primary sources provide valuable content information about a specific person, idea or trend, event, or place, among other things. To access that information, the student "enters" into the place and time being studied.

The teacher can design various scenarios to "place" students in the historical moment. Some examples are described later in this book. Aware of the subjective, incomplete nature of primary sources, students assess the source for accuracy, purpose, message, and point of view. How does the information offered compare to that provided by other primary and secondary sources? What message is the source sending? What opinion is the source expressing? The student gets to know the primary source, learning what it is and what it is not to gain its secrets.

As the above questions indicate, the learning process draws on prior knowledge and requires further study to make sense of the source and its content. Since primary sources tell incomplete stories, they act as one piece of a larger puzzle. Students construct the puzzle by consulting other sources to create a larger base of information and greater understanding of the topic of study.

An inquiry model provides the structure that makes learning happen. It guides students through a cycle of questions and answers that makes them responsible for their learning. Part of that responsibility requires making decisions based on evidence. Students not only need to develop conclusions, they also have to support those findings with pertinent supporting evidence. From the beginning to the end of the inquiry process, students are actively engaged in a complex set of skills exercises. As they learn content, students build important literacy and problem-solving skills.

Another related value concerns the increasing use of document-based questions (DBQ). The DBQ is becoming a regular assessment tool in classrooms and in standardized tests. They are also appearing more frequently as a classroom learning method. Primary sources are prominent documents in the DBQ.

On a practical level, having students familiar with primary sources and inquiry can improve assessment results. Regular classroom instruction using an inquiry model stressing primary source use means students will possess strong expertise when meeting the DBQ as an assessment. Students are evaluated on their knowledge, their ability to analyze sources, and their presentation of findings. If students are not familiar with inquiry, primary sources, and the DBQ process, the assessment is flawed. Instead of evaluating what students have learned, they are being tested on their ability to master a new method, the DBQ.

In conclusion, primary sources are valuable because they can act as the pivot around which learning revolves. The sources stimulate student interest and initiate the inquiry process. They act as major sources of information while their analysis actively engages students in building skills that facilitate learning content.

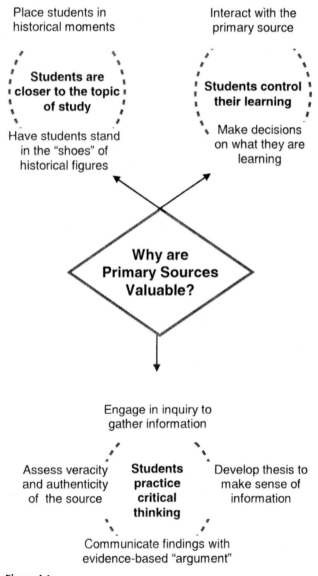

Figure I.1.
Author created

HOW HAS THE DIGITAL AGE
AFFECTED PRIMARY SOURCES?

The digital age has revolutionized primary sources as documents and how they are used in the classroom. As is generally true of many innovations, the digitizing of primary sources has had positive and negative consequences. A balance exists between the tremendous advances offered by the computer and the issues that these advances have raised. This mix of good and bad is evident in accessing sources, reading them, and regarding possible manipulation.

The Internet has totally transformed access. In predigital times, getting their hands on the sources was perhaps the biggest issue teachers and students faced. The textbook and primary source document readers provided the easiest access. But the amount and types of sources was limited.

Digitizing sources created an opposite situation. The click of a mouse puts millions of sources into our hands. Access is easy, but sifting through those millions to find the right one can be tedious and time-consuming. Interestingly, the change in access has not solved a perennial problem teachers face; namely, getting the right sources.

Digitization also has enhanced awareness of old concerns while raising new issues regarding the veracity and the authenticity of the sources. The ability to make a print document, a visual, or a motion picture into an electronic file is a mixed blessing. When viewed on a computer screen, digital copies can be much sharper and easier to read. Often, options exist that allow the reader to zoom into details in ways not possible with hard copies. For example, the Library of Congress has map software with a zoom function that can make even the smallest detail clearly visible.

An issue is that printouts and often projections lose resolution. They may become blurry. Reading the source on any format besides the digitized image on the computer screen may be difficult. Think of the difference in quality between an original and a photocopy.

Another downside is that digitization can increase the distance between the student and the source context. Looking at a primary source on a computer screen can lessen the ability of the source to place the student in the historical moment. The source becomes a virtual document rather than a real, physical artifact, even if it is a photocopy, held in your hand. This distance is not as big an issue with video, in which access can bring students closer to the historical moment or the place.

Manipulation is another issue. The practice of manipulating a primary source is not new. For example, photographers have staged scenes, moving people and objects around for various reasons. They also have altered images in the processing of photos. These alterations may involve making minor adjustments for clarity or major alterations that profoundly change the look of the document and its content.[1]

The big distinction in the digital age is that almost anyone can easily alter or radically transform an electronic document with the touch of a computer mouse. We are not referring to the ability to clean up a document or make it clearer. Here, the concern is about the manipulation of content that can create a distorted, inaccurate, and false document that thwarts student learning.

The lesson learned is that with digital documents, what you see is what you get. The caution is that what you get may or may not be a true replica of the original. Before using the document as a primary source authority, make sure the website is reliable and trustworthy. Check the source document, too.

DRAFTS, MULTIPLE VERSIONS, AND FINAL COPY

In many cases, differing versions of primary source documents exist. Using different versions of a document can highlight the dynamic quality of its creation, stressing the hard work and thought that went into perfecting the final product.

Print documents often go through a number of drafts and editing to produce the final copy. Whether it is a newspaper story, a magazine article, an email, or a memoir, editing creates different versions. Official documents in particular follow a process of drafts and revisions that lead to a final version. Before a bill in Congress becomes a law, a strict, careful scrutiny and revision process is mandated. Often the final bill that becomes law differs from the original introduced.

The U.S. Declaration of Independence is a famous example of how a document can change. In Thomas Jefferson's draft, King George III is criticized for encouraging the African slave trade.[2] The final version omits that condemnation.

Similarly, many visuals have several versions. Photographers often take several different pictures of a scene. In 1936, while working for the Farm Security Administration, Dorothea Lange took a series of pictures of thirty-two-year old Florence Thompson, a female migrant farm worker in California, and her children. Known as *Migrant Mother*, one photo became an iconic picture symbolizing the hard times of the Depression. That photo shows the mother and her children but gives little indication of their surroundings. The other pictures in the series show that they lived in a tent and that the tent was in a field. Looking at the series tells a fuller story of the family than the single *Migrant Mother* photo does.[3]

By examining different versions, students gain insight into the progression of ideas of the writer, photographer, artist, and others. They also may get a more complete portrayal and perhaps various perspectives of the document's subject.

In some cases, film and video in particular, but also regarding fine art, different media formats can be examined to trace development over time. The varied formats also can show differences in what is communicated and how the message is transmitted. Having students examine a screenplay and then view the movie or video offers them insight into the creative process. It also can translate into students producing their own works, moving perhaps from screenplay to video. A similar progression is evident from artist sketches to final product.

From a pragmatic standpoint, examining draft and final products allows students to see the progression of work that went into the various drafts or the differing options that were pursued. Hopefully, studying various versions can instill the idea that their own work needs similar editing and consideration. Just because a task is completed does not mean it is done—most often, the reverse is true.

STUDYING A PRIMARY SOURCE AS A TEXT

To be useful in the classroom, students need to be able to study the primary source as a text. Study requires being able to validate the legitimacy of the source document; to read the source for content; to ascertain the message, purpose, and bias; and to fit the source within the larger scope of study. The idea of a text is that it contains information of value that contributes to the learning process.

The following pages present a basic inquiry model for studying any primary source document that integrates the source securely within the learning process. No matter what size, shape, or type, there are certain basic criteria for studying a primary source.

But primary sources come in various sizes, shapes, and types. Each kind—indeed each source—has unique qualities that can influence how it is studied. So the basic model likely needs tinkering to fit the type and the specific source. It is important to note that the model presented below relates to the study of a single primary source document, not a more general inquiry model used to study a topic.

The basic inquiry model described here is as comprehensive as possible, meaning, in some cases, that questions may not apply to the study of the individual document. In other instances, they may need to be revised. Because a truly comprehensive model is almost impossible to construct, other questions might be added.

The context of the exercise determines what questions are asked. For example, a primary source can be used to open a unit or the study of a topic. It can be examined as part of an ongoing exploration of a topic. Or, a source can be studied at the end of the learning experience, possibly as part of an assessment. Each of these scenarios influences what questions are asked.

The inquiry model has six interrelated steps. The teacher's role depends upon student mastery of the model. As students gain expertise, the teacher's role should diminish.

Identity is the opening step and has the source introduce itself to the students by telling what it is, how it came about, and where it is from. This information is the provenance, the origin or pedigree of the source.

Context involves reading the source, the textbook, and possibly other sources to have students see the larger picture into which the source fits. First, students learn why and for whom it was created. Second, they set the source within its historical period and also begin the process of connecting it to the topic of study. Prior knowledge plays an important role here.

Content involves students opening up a dialogue with the source to learn the basic facts and its message. They pose questions and study the source to find answers. The strategy focuses on the question-and-answer cycle specifically used to study the source document.

Evaluation requires the student to assess the source, its information, and its message for accuracy, bias, and perspective (how the content delivers a specific point of view). Students examine what the source says and what it does not say. They note any inaccuracies or misleading statements.

Significance addresses a pivotal question: Why do we care? Consulting prior knowledge and other sources, students gauge the impact of the source at the time, in later periods, and on their own lives.

Connection occurs throughout the inquiry process but, most importantly, after studying the source. Students connect the source to the topic by relating what they learned from the document to what they already know, preparing them for further study. They also pose questions that its examination raised.

The Basic Primary Source Inquiry Model chart depicts the process.

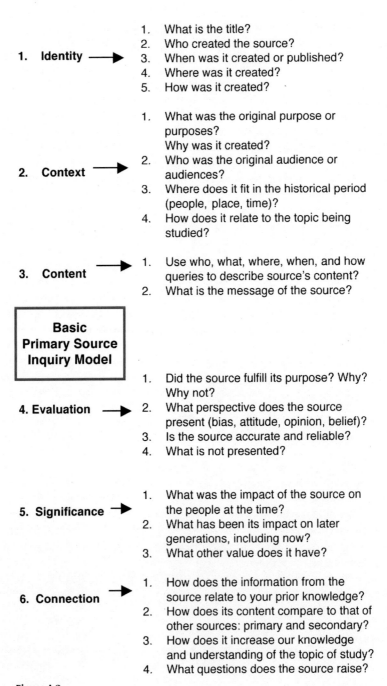

1. Identity ⟶
1. What is the title?
2. Who created the source?
3. When was it created or published?
4. Where was it created?
5. How was it created?

2. Context ⟶
1. What was the original purpose or purposes?
   Why was it created?
2. Who was the original audience or audiences?
3. Where does it fit in the historical period (people, place, time)?
4. How does it relate to the topic being studied?

3. Content ⟶
1. Use who, what, where, when, and how queries to describe source's content?
2. What is the message of the source?

Basic Primary Source Inquiry Model

4. Evaluation ⟶
1. Did the source fulfill its purpose? Why? Why not?
2. What perspective does the source present (bias, attitude, opinion, belief)?
3. Is the source accurate and reliable?
4. What is not presented?

5. Significance ⟶
1. What was the impact of the source on the people at the time?
2. What has been its impact on later generations, including now?
3. What other value does it have?

6. Connection ⟶
1. How does the information from the source relate to your prior knowledge?
2. How does its content compare to that of other sources: primary and secondary?
3. How does it increase our knowledge and understanding of the topic of study?
4. What questions does the source raise?

Figure I.2.
Author created

NOTES

1. The Detroit Publishing Company collection on The Henry Ford website offers a detailed description of how the company manipulated photographic images in the pre-digital era. See the "How Did They Do It?" pages at www.thehenryford.org/exhibits/dpc/how/special.asp, accessed January 26, 2014.

2. A reconstructed version of Thomas Jefferson's original draft of the Declaration of Independence is available on the Library of Congress website, www.loc.gov/exhibits/declara/ruffdrft.html, accessed January 26, 2014.

3. http://www.loc.gov/rr/print/list/128_migm.html, accessed January 26, 2014.

Part One

Understanding Primary Sources

THE WORLD OF PRIMARY SOURCES

Primary sources come in all shapes, sizes, and types. Because almost anything that provides firsthand, direct evidence can qualify as a primary source, attempting to catalog all of the varied types will probably fall short. The comprehensive range of primary sources encompasses all we are and all we have been. It also includes a similar span of what the natural environment is today and what it has been.

The World of Primary Sources chart below depicts the immense world of primary sources that teachers and students might use. To categorize the vast and diverse array of types, they have been organized into two large categories: human documents and physical remains. Human documents are divided into print, still visual, oral culture, and media. Each of these subcategories can be further broken down into more specific types. The "physical remains" subcategory focuses on aspects of the natural and built environment as well as all those material items that make up much of our everyday life. Here, too, subcategories can be further divided into more detailed types. The chart shows that the world of primary sources has both breadth and depth.

The pages that follow explore various types of sources. The objective is to provide as comprehensive as possible description of the diverse primary sources available. Knowing about each type facilitates effective use in the classroom. Knowing what comprises the world of primary sources provides teachers with a strong foundation. They can be more aware of the numerous options and possibilities. They can gain insight into similarities and differences. Knowing the world of primary sources sets the stage for planning their effective use in the classroom.

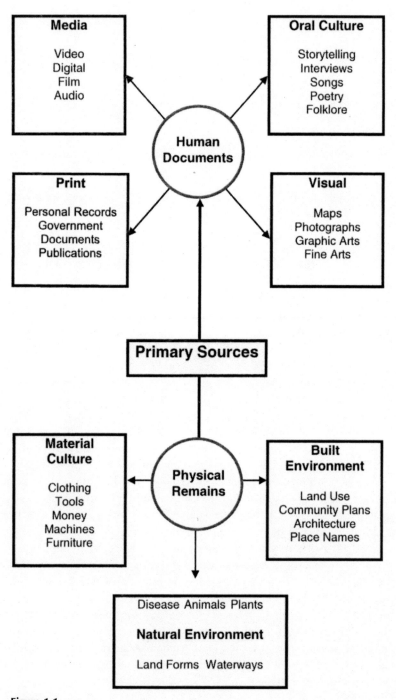

Figure 1.1.
Author created

PRINT DOCUMENTS: PAPER AND ELECTRONIC

Traditionally, print documents have been the most used type of primary source in the classroom. They are the largest and most easily accessed body of primary sources. Omnipresent and pervading virtually every aspect of public and personal life, they reflect the high value our literate society places on the written word. This value also is shown by the strong movement to improve reading in schools.

To a great extent, three technological advances fueled the proliferation of print sources. The printing press mechanized the production of written works, leading to the mass dissemination of a wide variety of publications. Beyond the obvious impetus to expanding literacy the printing press provided, it also exponentially increased the number and variety of publications available to contemporary and later audiences. A related consequence was that the printing press largely eliminated handwritten books. But it did not do away with other handwritten personal correspondence or versions of government and business documents. Though it was published on a printing press, Thomas Jefferson wrote the Declaration of Independence using pen and paper.[1]

The second innovation was the typewriter in the late 1800s. It served as a transition from hand to mechanical writing. The typewriter continued the erosion of handwritten documents that reached fruition with the computer. It also provided the means to create a rich store of easily read paper documents.

If the typewriter acted as a transition phase in written communication, the computer represents a culmination. In many instances, it has eliminated most handwritten documents and replaced the typewriter, which has now become a mechanical relic of an earlier age. It also has lessened the need for a physical product. Most communication previously done on paper is conducted electronically and, often, there is no paper trail, just an electronic signature, so to speak. Equally important, communication has been exponentially accelerated so as to seem instantaneous. Typing, sending, and receiving can be combined into a single process, enabled by the click of a computer mouse. The ease of communication has created a situation in which every day, we can be bombarded with all sorts of electronic documents, such as emails and PDFs (portable document format). In addition, cell phones have further expanded print communication via text messages.

In many ways, digital documents are similar to paper. A major difference is the electronic medium, though a digital source can be printed out on paper and a paper document can be scanned into a digital format. What has not changed is the nature of the print document. No matter if it is paper or digital, students need to question the document, not take what it says at face value.

Appearing in print does not make a primary source objective truth. As is true of every primary source, no matter what type it is, each print document has its own story to tell from its own perspective. In addition, the story fits a certain format. It is presented within a conventional structure and is told using a particular vocabulary and grammar that determines not only what is related but also how it is related and what is included as well as what is omitted.

A personal letter differs substantially from a business letter in structure, tone, and, obviously, content. Similarly, a newspaper story adheres to different rules than an editorial. The story purports to report the news as objectively as possible, while the editorial's express purpose is commentary.

Perspective and type influence what is and is not included in the document. Many times, the most important question to ask is: What is missing from the source? That question provides teachers with a strong opportunity to promote student learning.

Print documents have the unique quality of opening windows into private and public life. When students study multiple documents of various types, such as a newspaper account, a diary entry, and a government report, they gain a full-bodied, multidimensional portrait of an event, a person, or a place. Since the documents provide varying points of view presented in different ways, students meet information that may confirm or conflict with that presented in other sources. As is true of all primary sources, students learn that a print document only yields its secrets and opens a window on life when they study it with a critical, questioning eye.

An obvious prerequisite to effective use in the classroom is student ability to read the source. In many cases, the language, the vocabulary, and the structure raise obstacles to student reading. Though the Declaration of Independence is a cornerstone document in U.S. history and has value as an example of classical rhetoric, its language may be above the reading level of the elementary grades and possibly middle and high school students. The dilemma teachers face is whether to use the original document, sacrificing student comprehension, versus rewriting the document to use language students can understand, sacrificing the authenticity of the original. A rewritten Declaration is not a primary source document, but that does not mean rewriting should not be considered.

Perhaps the best option is for teachers to provide the original for students to see, so they get a sense of the document. Then, either supply a glossary of terms or rewrite the document in grade-appropriate language. In many cases, only excerpts of the primary source are studied. Here, too, having the full original available for students to see offers them insight into the source.

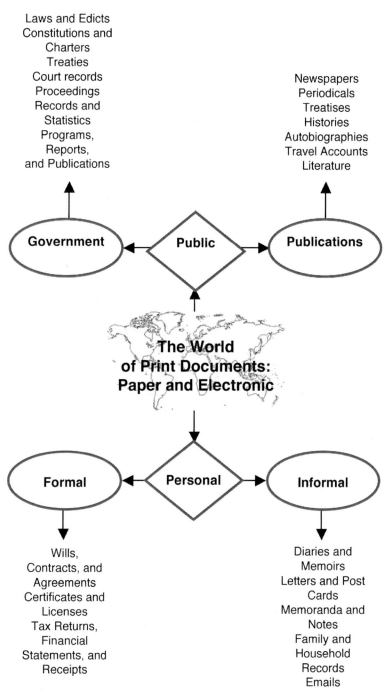

Laws and Edicts
Constitutions and
Charters
Treaties
Court records
Proceedings
Records and
Statistics
Programs,
Reports,
and Publications

Newspapers
Periodicals
Treatises
Histories
Autobiographies
Travel Accounts
Literature

Government

Public

Publications

The World
of Print Documents:
Paper and Electronic

Formal

Personal

Informal

Wills,
Contracts, and
Agreements
Certificates and
Licenses
Tax Returns,
Financial
Statements, and
Receipts

Diaries and
Memoirs
Letters and Post
Cards
Memoranda and
Notes
Family and
Household
Records
Emails

Figure 1.2.
Author created; world outline image is PD

VISUAL DOCUMENTS

Reflecting the increasing presence of visual images in everyday life, visual primary sources are becoming more prominent in the classroom. They are as diverse as print documents and almost as ubiquitous. While visual images share some common qualities, each type has distinct characteristics, including unique composition conventions that influence how the image looks and what is or is not included.

The focus here is on static visual images. Motion images are explored under film/video. Like print primary sources, visual images can have a physical or digital format. The same cautions noted for digital print documents apply to digital visual images.

Visual primary sources come in two general categories. First, there are types that appear to be reproduced reality, such as photographs. Second, other types are facsimiles created by people either by hand or other means. Some of these representations also may seem faithful and accurate, such as maps. Others, such as cartoons or paintings, are purposely expressive in their content.

Visual primary sources are slippery documents. Often perceived to be objective, accurate reflections of reality, they are expressive documents that send a specific message. Visual primary sources generally combine elements of reality with cultural and perhaps personal attitudes or beliefs. The visuals show us how a person and often a culture perceived a place, an event, a person, or a people. These pictures reflect contemporary attitudes, beliefs, and opinions. They can use composition conventions and means of production that showcase the aesthetics and the technology of the society.[2] The culture that produced a map sketched on a clay tablet with a reed stylus obviously differed from one that drew a map by hand, or a culture that produced it on a computer. This example highlights an important aspect of primary source study. Style and modes of production also are important considerations.

The big issue for students is their visual literacy competency. A picture might be worth a thousand words, but for students to get that value, they need to know how a visual works, how to read it, and how to interpret what was read. Reading visuals follows a path similar to reading print. Students identify provenance, highlight important content, evaluate the message and purpose, and more.

Visuals generally, and each visual type has its own grammar, so to speak. Student familiarity with the type of visual and its nature as well as the composition conventions that guide its creation can facilitate the reading. Much as students often learn to write a print document, such as a letter or report, so having them learn how to draw a map or to take a photograph using professional techniques provides them with important insight into the visual.

Another important consideration for teachers is that visuals have been shown to be effective educational resources for second-language learners and students with special needs.[3]

To further explore how visual primary sources work, three major types are profiled in the following pages: maps, photographs, and editorial cartoons.

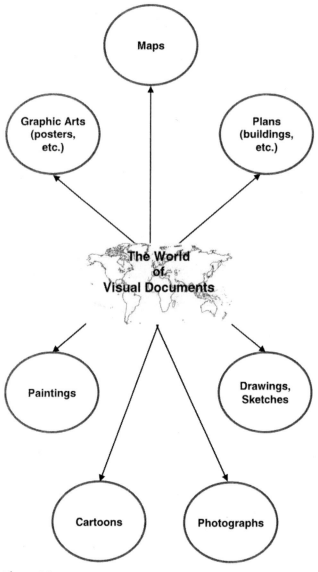

Figure 1.3.
Author created; world outline image is PD

MAPS

Maps are familiar resources in history and social studies courses. In most cases, reference maps are used to identify landforms, waterways, continents, nations, states, and cities, among other places. Cartographic elements, symbols, and scales help students to locate places, to plot locations, to measure distances, and to perform other basic map exercises.

The first lesson for students is to recognize that maps come in various styles and types and are created out of sundry materials. Using numerous graphic styles, maps have been drawn on clay tablets, stone, papyrus, parchment, and paper, as well as other materials. Most recently, computers have been used to draw electronic versions of maps.

For example, historical primary source maps are beginning to be used more frequently in classrooms. They often look very different from modern reference maps and can serve different purposes. While modern maps tend to be as scientifically drawn as possible, that is not true of all historical maps. They do not necessarily help us locate places or show us how to get from here to there. The European *mappamundi* (world map) of the medieval period provided a religious view of the world from the perspective of Christianity. One purpose was to serve as a "road map" to salvation.[4] In addition, historical maps feature different projections than current maps and can picture the world in unfamiliar ways. As primary sources, old maps are valuable because they illuminate important aspects of a culture in ways other documents do not.

Primary sources maps often offer a visual portrait of a culture, mixing cultural perspectives with elements of reality to depict themselves and others.[5]

Lesson two is understanding that the nature of maps requires students to examine them with a wary eye. A common misperception is that maps are scientifically plotted, objective, and accurate depictions. As the above discussion indicates, they are not. Maps are a creative and often artistic means of picturing information. No map can include all the information needed to totally and accurately show its subject. Pragmatic concerns and cartographic conventions combine with cultural attitudes and beliefs to create the map. As a result, maps integrate elements of reality with personal and cultural attitudes and beliefs. They are subjective and incomplete by nature. Even classroom reference maps have their inherent biases since they include or omit information. Many reference maps show countries of the world but leave out geographic features or vice versa. This does not mean they are wrong, just that they have a specific purpose.

The very making of a map is a subjective exercise. Transforming a three-dimensional subject into a two-dimensional depiction involves making decisions on what projection to use, how the map is oriented (what is at the top), the scale of distances and sizes, and, among other things, what symbols and colors to use. Another decision concerns what content to include and what is left out. The map only contains what is known at the time and place of creation. Before 1492, all world maps from Europe, Asia, and Africa left out an entire hemisphere.

The purpose of the map influences how the various elements come together to send its message. The Mercator projection was originally created in the sixteenth century to aid navigation. By design, it flattened the world to project a more even grid, vastly expanding the size of the northern hemisphere in the process. Over time, the Mercator projection became standard and was used for other purposes, including school maps. Those using the map thought it accurately depicted the earth. But by enhancing Europe and the northern hemisphere, the Mercator map became a graphic statement of European supremacy. Later projections corrected the distortions of the Mercator projection. Europe and North America shrunk in size, while Africa, in particular, greatly increased.[6]

Another aspect of many maps that shows their subjective nature concerns what is in the center. The oldest existing world map from Babylon ca. 1500 BCE has Babylon in the center. The European *mappamundi* reflected the religious emphasis of the time, having Jerusalem in the center.

A third consideration is the map's orientation. Is north up? Most maps have north on the top, creating the impression that north is up. Actually, north is a relative orientation. Islamic maps often have Mecca in the center and can be oriented with south to the top.[7]

As a result, using maps as primary sources can require teachers and students to rethink what maps are and what their nature is.

Recent technological innovations have created new opportunities for using old maps in the classroom. Digitization has created electronic versions of thousands of historic maps that were previously difficult or impossible to obtain. They are now readily accessible. When viewed on a computer screen, enhanced resolution makes these maps easy to read. In addition, as noted in the introduction, some online archives such as the Library of Congress website have software that allows viewers to navigate around maps and bird's-eye views as well as to zoom into details. Students can zoom into the digital version of the 1507 Martin Waldseemuller world map to see the word *America* printed in modern-day South America. This map represented the first time the western hemisphere was called America. The name reflected mapmaker Waldseemuller's admiration for explorer Amerigo Vespucci. That is how America got its name.[8]

Technology also has profoundly affected current mapping. Satellite imagery and geographic information systems (GIS) have provided a wealth of geographic information that has been translated into maps. In this context, maps have become a vehicle for managing and organizing massive amounts of information.

Cartogram
Map showing statistical data in comparative relationship.

Fire Insurance
Maps of urban areas and buildings. Note construction and other materials. Drawn for insurance companies.

Bird's-Eye View
Image of an area or community from a high oblique angle perspective looking down.

Cadastral
Map showing land boundaries, often to show property titles.

Portolan Chart
Medieval European nautical charts. Drawn on Vellum.

Sample Map Projection Formats

GIS
Geographic Information System map digitally created using data systems.

Plat
Simple map often drawn by a surveyor to define land titles.

T-O
Used before 1492. Shows round world, water surrounds landmasses that are divided by two rivers into three areas, often signifying Africa, Asia, Europe.

Ptolemaic
Used before 1492. Developed by Ptolemy in Alexandria. Plots world on mathematical grid. Omits Americas, connects Africa to Asia, making Indian Ocean inland sea.

Sample World Map Projection Formats

Mercator
Developed by Gerhard Mercator to aid ships in plotting courses. Became popular projection, but distorts size of northern hemisphere.

Figure 1.4.

Author created; world outline image is PD

PHOTOGRAPHS

Thanks to cameras in cell phones and other handheld devices, photographs have become even more engrained in everyday life than they were in the past. With the touch of a button and a click of a computer mouse, we can take, store, manipulate, and send photos to other people. The camera has become almost an extension of our eyes. We see something interesting, we snap a picture, and it is saved for posterity. As this guide is being written, the current vogue is "selfies," self-portraits taken with our cell phones. Equally important, digitized collections have amazingly expanded access to photographs taken in the past and present from all over the globe.

For all the hype about other media, photographs remain the go-to visual for the vast majority of people.

As primary sources, photographs are extremely valuable but also very risky documents. A misconception many people hold is that photographs are objective mirrors of reality, that they are truthful. Certainly, elements of reality are included in photographs, but how they are framed, how they are shown, and what is not included work against the truth perception. Pioneering documentary photography, Lewis Hine made the famous statement in 1906 that while photos do not lie, photographers might.[9]

Lying is too strong a word. Photography is an expressive medium, an art as well as a documentary form. Each photo has a specific purpose and message to send. The idea that photos are authentic, accurate, and neutral frozen moments in time is like a photograph itself. That idea tells an incomplete story from a well-defined perspective.

The photo is less a mirror of reality than an expressive, realistic image of what the camera lens captured. The photograph results from the complex interworking of factors that are further complicated by what people bring to viewing the photo. The technology of the camera and the processing of the image; the purpose; the conventions applied to compose the scene; and the perspectives of the photographer, the subject, and the viewer come together to create the photographic experience.

Although photos are two-dimensional representations, they invite inquiry from multiple perspectives. Their value is that we must learn not just to look at the photos, but also to see them from various points of view to interpret their messages.

What you see is not what you get when looking at a photo. Rather, what you get is what you see, and that can vary among different people. The photographer composes the scene to send the message that may be enhanced in the processing of the image. The subject(s) may have had a similar or different idea of the photo's purpose. Armed with their individual ideas, attitudes, and ability to read the photo, viewers may get the message or perceive something different from the photo.[10] In these ways, photographs help define what is meant by saying visual primary sources are slippery.

Because photos are so familiar and present in everyday life, teaching students to study them almost seems unnecessary. It is needed. Learning how a photographer composes a scene provides students with valuable insight and also gives them a strategy for studying photos. Photographers manipulate to create a better, more pleasing picture.

Generally, photographers use the rule of thirds to compose photographs. They divide the scene horizontally and vertically by thirds, creating a grid. The photo has a foreground, a subject, and a background, providing a three-dimensional feel. The framing determines what is and is not shown in the photo as well as what the focus is. Borrowed from painting, the rule of thirds provides photos with perspective, adding an artistic component to photography.[11]

EDITORIAL CARTOONS

Editorial cartoons offer sharp commentary on people, places, and events, among other things. They appear in newspapers, magazines, or on websites, but they also might be independently produced and distributed. While cartoons are often satirical, comic, or ironic, many are deadly serious in their portrayals. What they all have in common is that they exaggerate their subject matter to send the message. The exaggeration often helps elicit an emotional response in viewers.[12]

The nature of editorial cartoons is to educate and to persuade. They try to make viewers feel, think, and often act. Editorial cartoons try to persuade us to accept a certain point of view. But the subjectivity of cartoons extends far beyond exaggeration. Artistic and economic considerations are also important and are closely related.

As a work of art, the editorial cartoon is an expressive medium. It expresses the opinion of various people involved in the creation and publication of the cartoon, including the publisher, editor, possibly an author, and, of course, the cartoonist. In some cases, the cartoon stands alone. In other instances, it accompanies a written piece such as an editorial, article, or other item. The end result meshes artistry with a political, economic, cultural, personal, or other perspective that accentuates the subjective quality of the cartoon.

The exaggerated focus also means much is omitted from the picture. Generally consisting of an individual image or scene, many cartoons send a single message. In some cases, that message is straightforward, offering a one-dimensional opinion on a topic. Other cartoons are more sophisticated.

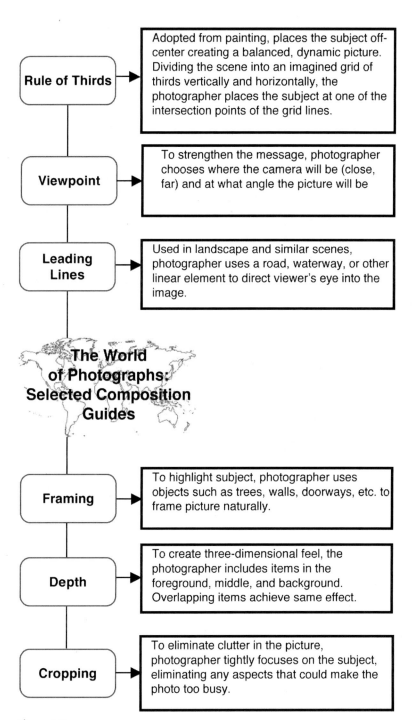

Rule of Thirds → Adopted from painting, places the subject off-center creating a balanced, dynamic picture. Dividing the scene into an imagined grid of thirds vertically and horizontally, the photographer places the subject at one of the intersection points of the grid lines.

Viewpoint → To strengthen the message, photographer chooses where the camera will be (close, far) and at what angle the picture will be

Leading Lines → Used in landscape and similar scenes, photographer uses a road, waterway, or other linear element to direct viewer's eye into the image.

The World of Photographs: Selected Composition Guides

Framing → To highlight subject, photographer uses objects such as trees, walls, doorways, etc. to frame picture naturally.

Depth → To create three-dimensional feel, the photographer includes items in the foreground, middle, and background. Overlapping items achieve same effect.

Cropping → To eliminate clutter in the picture, photographer tightly focuses on the subject, eliminating any aspects that could make the photo too busy.

Figure 1.5.
Author created; world outline image is PD

Instead of overtly presenting a point of view, they try to make us pose questions. Often, the answers to the questions lead us to the cartoonist's predetermined conclusion.

Economic concerns are foundational elements of cartoons. One basic function of the cartoon is to promote the artist. In turn, the cartoonist can act as a draw for a publication, attracting new readers and keeping existing readers as subscribers. As a marketing tool, the cartoon typically supplies a visual representation that expresses the political beliefs and attitudes of the publication and its readers. In this respect, editorial cartoons combine art and economics. They provide commentary and promote the work and career of the cartoonist.

Many visuals include captions that provide context or content. Photos often have captions, and so do cartoons. The combination of picture and words is geared to strengthen the message, making certain that viewers actually get it. In some cases, the caption is the central communication medium, while the cartoon is used to illustrate the point being made. In other instances, the reverse is true.

The interplay of pictures and words offers teachers ideas on using cartoons in the classroom.

FILM/VIDEO

Motion pictures are a comparatively recent invention. Their creation was an international collaboration of sorts in the late nineteenth century. Three early pioneers were Eadweard Muybridge from England, Thomas Edison from the United States, and Louis Lumière from France.[13] As is true of their still picture relatives, film and video have become ubiquitous presences in our lives. Motion pictures are an incredibly versatile medium serving public and private purposes. They provide entertainment, report the news, and are used for advertising. They are used in education and act as an expressive art medium. Film/video also documents life, including family moments, among other things.

A stark difference exists between still and moving pictures. Film and video add important time dimensions. All media capture the past. But photos, maps, and others stop time, depicting a particular, singular, present moment. We have no inkling of what came before or after. While the same is true of motion pictures, they also show passage of time. In many instances, we see what happened in real time. As the action unfolds, the movement of past, present, and future is glimpsed. Motion provides a dynamic quality to the visuals. Because they are always in motion, film and video have a future orientation. We may anticipate what comes next rather than focus on what is being seen now.

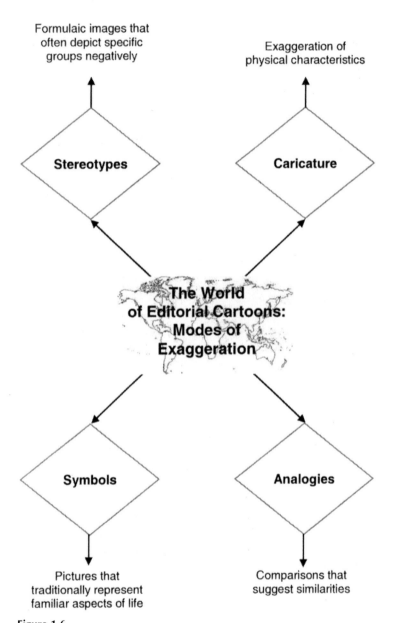

Formulaic images that often depict specific groups negatively

Exaggeration of physical characteristics

Stereotypes

Caricature

The World of Editorial Cartoons: Modes of Exaggeration

Symbols

Analogies

Pictures that traditionally represent familiar aspects of life

Comparisons that suggest similarities

Figure 1.6.
Author created; world outline image is PD

As is true of all media, film/video have a structure that can help students use these resources as learning texts. Following Aristotle's *Poetics*, professional motion pictures have a beginning, middle, and end.[14] These three parts are divided into scenes, much as a play has acts and scenes within each act. Each scene also has a beginning, middle, and end with the end either closing the action or both closing action and transitioning to the next scene. In a sense, a scene is a minimovie. Short videos may consist of one scene, while longer productions can have several scenes. A feature-length movie has between fifty and seventy scenes.

As is true of primary sources generally, film and video are expressive media that tell a story from a certain perspective. Even when chronicling reality, the story delivers a well-defined message.

Understanding the structure of motion pictures provides a clear guide to their study. Virtually all films and videos can be broken down into two types of scenes. Master scenes are larger organizational units. They resemble book chapters and generally have a beginning, middle, and end, although the end may be a transition to the next master scene. Within each master scene, smaller, more detailed scenes unfold to tell the story. These smaller scenes contain specific parts of the action, acting like sections within a chapter. Within each scene, action related to the topic of the scene tells its story.

Surveying the entire motion picture allows students to get a sense of the whole and to figure out the various scenes. Focusing on the scenes makes it is easier to accommodate the continual movement of the images and to study the content in depth.

The motion quality of film and video can present challenges to using them as primary sources in the classroom.[15] Because the action never stops, teachers need to provide questions prior to screening to prompt students on what to look for in the film/video. It is likely that more than one screening will be needed to get the full benefit of studying the film/video. Longer productions can raise several issues. Time is an obvious concern. How much time can be devoted to a single production?

As artistic productions, films and videos are created to tell a story in its entirety. To gain the maximum benefit of the film/video, it should be viewed from beginning to end. But the time issue often clashes with the artistic need for full viewing. Screening longer productions requires breaking up a film or video into smaller segments shown over several days. Shorter films/videos of perhaps twenty to thirty minutes likely consume an entire class period or more.

In addition, the longer the production, the more likely it will require greater prescreening instruction, closer attention during viewing over an extended time, and substantial postscreening to make sense of what was seen. Given the crowded curriculum of most history and social studies courses, full screenings are difficult to plan.

Equally important, questions, major points of interest, and other matters arise during the viewing of the film/video. If the screening is not halted to discuss important aspects, a prime learning moment is missed. As a result, and these suggestions are not necessarily the optimum solutions, either the production is stopped at critical times for discussion or important excerpts are shown.

The master scene provides teachers with the best option for stopping and starting or selecting excerpts. The scenario is similar to having students read chapters rather than a whole book. Over time, as students become more familiar with the motion picture medium and more expert at reading and interpreting a film/video, they probably can study longer productions effectively in shorter periods of time.

As is true of most primary sources, the computer can play an important role in using film/video as a primary source. The Internet supplies easy access to numerous productions while the computer screen offers high-resolution viewing and, if needed, individualized viewing. Students can view a film/video at their own pace, easily toggling back and forth as required to better study the production. Teachers can maximize the use of time by having students view film/video inside and outside class. They can get students started on reading and possibly interpreting a film/video in class and let them complete the study on their own.

In addition, sites such as YouTube include historic videos as well as current professional and amateur productions. These sites have vastly expanded access to a wide variety of videos on numerous topics. Often the videos are brief and tightly focused on a specific topic, facilitating study.

FINE ARTS

The fine arts bring an aesthetic quality to the study of history. They include painting, sculpture, statuary, prints, textiles, decorative arts, ceramics, metal works, and furniture. The fine arts serve as valuable cultural artifacts that can open doors into a society's ideas, beliefs, and attitudes. They often depict aspects of everyday life, the natural and the built environment, political figures, and war that offer insight into everyday life, religion, government, economics, and conflict, among other things. Fine arts can serve as barometers of change, depict cross-cultural influences, and deliver political messages.

Studying the fine arts moves beyond the work itself to other areas. The artists serve as valuable subjects for study, as do the patrons, whether they are

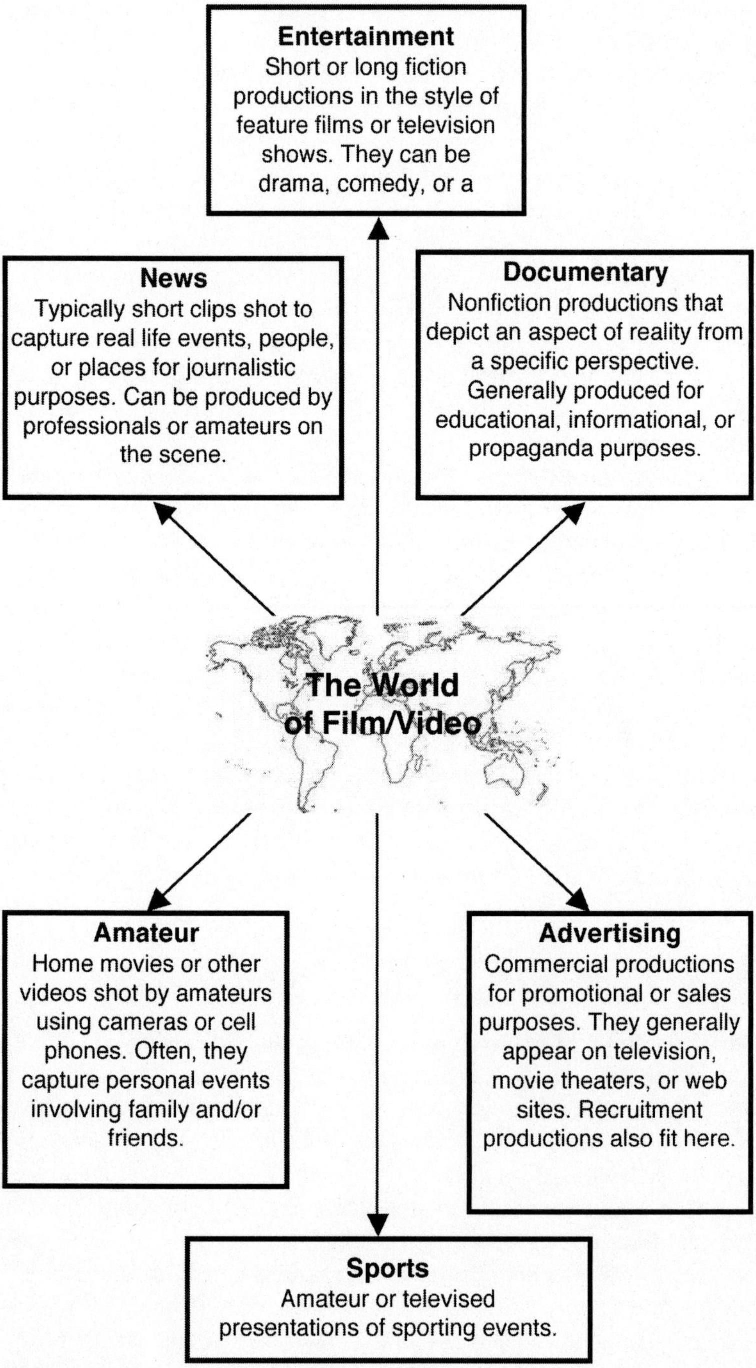

Entertainment
Short or long fiction
productions in the style of
feature films or television
shows. They can be
drama, comedy, or a

News
Typically short clips shot to
capture real life events, people,
or places for journalistic
purposes. Can be produced by
professionals or amateurs on
the scene.

Documentary
Nonfiction productions that
depict an aspect of reality from
a specific perspective.
Generally produced for
educational, informational, or
propaganda purposes.

**The World
of Film/Video**

Amateur
Home movies or other
videos shot by amateurs
using cameras or cell
phones. Often, they
capture personal events
involving family and/or
friends.

Advertising
Commercial productions
for promotional or sales
purposes. They generally
appear on television,
movie theaters, or web
sites. Recruitment
productions also fit here.

Sports
Amateur or televised
presentations of sporting events.

Figure 1.7.
Author created; world outline image is PD

private individuals or groups, religious organizations, businesses, or public agencies. Patronage can involve commissioning a work of art or purchasing it. Either way, exploring who supported fine arts in a society can offer insight into what was valued. The subjects of the artwork, the kinds of work supported, and where the works were displayed allow students to evaluate the status and role of art in the society.

Often, the subjects of the artwork show what a contemporary culture valued.[16] The sustained or shifting popularity of old and new styles helps increase the understanding of change and continuity. Studying the works of Michelangelo and other Renaissance artists offer insight into the influence of classical learning, the humanistic philosophy, and religion, among other things, during that era. Comparing those works to the generally religious-oriented works created in Europe during medieval times provides a stark contrast between those two ages.

The role art played in reflecting the rise of technology and industrialism is evident in the works of numerous artists, including Claude Monet, Marcel Duchamps, and Nam June Paik, to name just a few. Andy Warhol's art drives home the importance of advertising in our lives.

Similarly, art often has a strong political edge. The paintings of Jacques-Louis David evoke the revolutionary fervor of the French Revolution. Soviet and recent Chinese art often reflect political party doctrines. Dissent also is a prime subject of art. George Caleb Bingham commented wryly on the Jacksonian age in some of his paintings.[17]

Comparing artworks from different cultures can highlight differences, show similarities, and help assess cross-cultural connections. Comparing Hellenistic and contemporary Indian sculpture is a good example. Equally important, the fine arts have influenced other visual media. Photography's rule of thirds was borrowed from painting.

Studying a work of art can prove challenging to students. Close reading strategies can help demystify the process. Many art educators use a technique that differs from the traditional historical strategy that places the primary source in its people, place, and time context and establishes its provenance before examining content. This approach stresses teaching students to look at a work of art for an extended period of time. The study may be prefaced by the introduction or review of art composition characteristics, such as line, shape, and texture.

For several minutes, students study an artwork silently without knowing the title, artist, or other information, focusing on what they see. The teacher then probes the students to identify what they saw. Frequently, students see different things in a painting, so the discussion acts as a discovery exercise. Details can be pointed out, leading some students to exclaim, "Now I see it."

The content reading is followed by another close examination to make inferences about time, place, people, school of art, and other aspects related to the topic of study. An important aspect of this examination is having students support their inferences by referring to the artwork. The last stage involves identifying the artwork, the artist, and other relevant information, comparing it to what was already discovered.

The close reading technique helps students hone their observation and critical-thinking skills. It also allows them to gain a greater appreciation of fine art as a primary source and an educational resource. This technique can be applied to other primary sources when the need to improve reading and thinking skills is a primary objective.

Much as is true of other primary source types, technology has influenced the ability of teachers to use fine art as a primary source. Online access to museums vastly expands the types and the number of artworks available for study.

The computer screen offers high-resolution viewing. The caveat is that many artworks have textural and other elements that are not evident on the computer or in the various reproductions appearing in books, for example. Studying the original greatly enhances the viewing experience and the value of study. Especially if an interactive, close-reading session is included, planning a field trip to an art museum is well worth the time, the effort, and the expense.

FOLK CULTURE AND MYTHOLOGY

Often overlooked and unknown, folk culture and mythology provide an exceptionally rich and diverse body of primary sources. Encompassing all aspects of life of a specific people, folk culture includes:

- oral culture: creation and other tales, proverbs, and epic poetry
- material culture: crafts, clothes making, quilting, furniture and home building
- customs: rituals, ceremonies, foodways, family traditions
- performance arts: dance, music and song, games

What does folk culture do? In his article, "The Functions of Folklore," William Bascom provided four roles or purposes that relate to folk culture generally. Identifying amusement as a function, Bascom suggests that beneath humor is a deeper meaning related to societal pressure. Amusement helps relieve frustration. It also offers wry, satiric or ironic, and telling commentary on societal matters.

The remaining three functions have more general cultural applications. A second purpose is to validate aspects of culture, providing justification and,

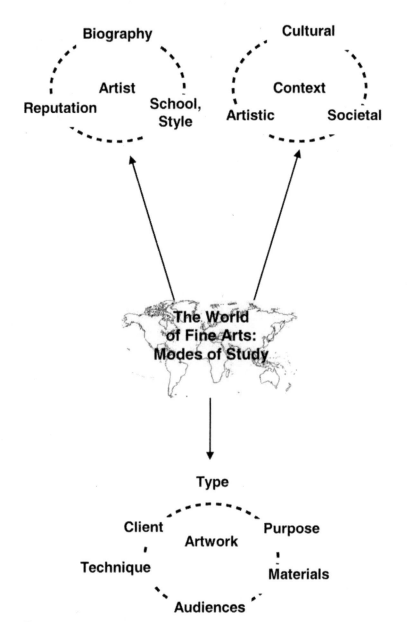

Figure 1.8.
Author created; world outline image is PD

perhaps, a guide to various rituals and social structure. Education is the third function. Maintaining conformity to accepted patterns of behavior is the fourth purpose. As Bascom explained, "More than simply serving to validate or justify institutions, beliefs and attitudes, some forms of folklore are important as means of applying social pressure and exercising social control."[18]

Folk culture is the traditional modes of behavior and expression of a people that are transmitted by firsthand interaction from one generation to another. In many ways, folk culture provides people with a sense of identity. It offers the ways and means to maintain tradition and to transmit history, cultural beliefs, and skills to succeeding generations. The functions of folklore can be easily transferred to the study of modern society, and so can the ideas that define folk culture.

Defining folk is an important first step in using the vast array of primary sources in the classroom. The term *folk* refers to the cultural aspects, beliefs, and attitudes of a specific group of a people or society. It often is applied to local, isolated peoples generally living in rural areas. What distinguishes a traditional culture from a modern one is somewhat vague, but two distinctions are oral versus written modes of communication and memory as well as handmade versus mechanized, industrial production. In many cases, folk describes past societies or current peoples who maintain ways of life rooted in past traditions.[19]

By studying folk culture, students gain unique insight into the inner beliefs and workings of a people. Beyond the content, the uses and the performance aspects also can prove illuminating. For example, certain African cultures have used proverbs in legal decisions to both determine court cases and explain the rationale behind the decisions.[20]

Regarding performance, several studies have shown that audience responses have influenced the length of folk tales and songs. The more enthusiastic the audience was, the longer the tale or song. Storytellers and singers were able to adapt their performances to audience responses because they did not memorize songs so much as mentally store a wide collection of lyric phrases, couplets, and more that they used as needed in performance. For example, many early blues singers memorized a large collection of verses that they drew upon to craft songs for specific audiences.[21] The same process seems to have been used by ancient Greek epic poets whose works may have helped create the body of stories that Homer wrote as the *Iliad* and *Odyssey*.[22]

Folk culture also includes specific methods of production of various everyday items and structures. Different peoples used different techniques to build houses, to make tools, or to decorate structures. Log cabins were a distinctive style of housing that Scandinavian pioneers brought to the Americas during colonial times.[23] Pottery, basketry, and clothing also have defined a people. Many ancient cultures are named for their distinctive pottery. In some cases, spear points are used to identify a people, such as the pre-Columbian Clovis culture. Clovis refers to a certain type of spear point found by archaeologists in Clovis, New Mexico.[24] Gender roles, courting and marriage, and rites of passage are other cultural aspects that characterize a people.

An intriguing but overlooked aspect of culture study generally is food-ways. The old saying "you are what you eat" aptly describes the value of looking at cuisine. Very little says more about a people and a culture than their food and drink. Today, we often identify food with a specific people: fish and chips with the English, sushi with the Japanese. In other cases, food connects to various regions. Among many other examples that could be cited, in the United States, clam chowder brings to mind the Northeast, Tex-Mex the Southwest, and the South with grits. The Mediterranean region has a specific diet that is considered to be very healthy. And some holidays have their traditional foods. Thanksgiving means turkey and sweet potatoes to millions of Americans.

Religion also influences foodways. Among many Jewish families, the Passover holiday requires a change of diet to replicate the food available to the Hebrews escaping Egypt in biblical times, especially matzo or unleavened bread. Most Christians observe Lent, the forty-day period before Easter, by eliminating the eating of meat and any meat by-products, except milk and eggs, on specific days of abstinence. Similarly, during the month of Ramadan, Muslims follow religious guidelines on fasting.

Sometimes, religious doctrine prohibits certain foods. The Hindu religion bans the eating of beef, while both Judaism and Islam forbid eating pork.

In addition, some foods that are currently connected to certain places resulted from cultural interaction, especially the Columbian exchange of people, animals, plants, disease, and ideas that occurred following Christopher Columbus's 1492 voyage. Some familiar dishes are prime examples. Few foods are more American than hot dogs and apple pie. Hot dogs came to the United States with immigrants from Frankfurt, Germany, thus the name *frankfurters*. Apples originated in central Asia. Pasta with red sauce is considered an Italian staple, but that dish synthesizes two important exchanges. Pasta originated in China and purportedly was brought to Italy by Marco Polo. Tomatoes came to Europe from the Americas as part of the Columbian exchange.[25]

Not only cuisine but also preparation and cookware offer insight into a culture and into cultural exchange. In some cases, food preparation involves an intricate cultural ritual. Luaus are traditional Hawaiian celebrations featuring specific ways of cooking the meal. The pig is the centerpiece of the luau, but it is not indigenous to the islands. Rather, Polynesian settlers brought the pig to Hawaii.

Cookware also is an important primary source. The wok is basic to most East Asian and Southeast Asian food. The fork was brought to Europe from China.

In the classroom, the obvious way to study food is to prepare it in the traditional way with traditional cookware and then eat it, perhaps using traditional utensils. Since actual experience is not always possible, recipes, pictures, and written accounts can be studied.

Mythology is an aspect of folk culture that needs a separate explanation. Often considered to be fiction or tall tales, for our purposes, mythology is defined as oral traditions that explain and validate cultural customs, norms, and history as well as to provide guidance to maintain conformity of behavior or permit behavioral deviance. Myths can help explain creation or life and death. They can establish the origins, purposes, and practices of religion and magic. Some myths confirm aspects of a people's purpose, destiny, and values. In the context of a primary source, myth means a traditional story that relates the early history of a people or explains a phenomenon.

Creation stories represent one of the best-known forms of mythology. Some stories explain the origins of the world and people. Others extend to explanation of such natural phenomena as the seasons and weather. In Greek mythology, thunder is explained as the god Zeus throwing thunderbolts when angry. Among Native Americans, coyote is a trickster figure. The stories featuring coyote often explain natural phenomenon and human characteristics.[26] Both the characters and the narrative of the myths illuminate the central values, attitudes, and beliefs of a people.

A caveat is that while creation stories were originally oral traditions, most have been written down. The versions we have available may reflect changes that occurred over time, possibly to better fit the written media structure and grammar.

Another important feature of folk culture and mythology is that it transcends traditional disciplinary bounds. History, English/language arts, anthropology, and psychology can be combined to study an aspect of folk culture. Together, these disciplines provide teachers and students with a multidimensional inquiry model to study a people.

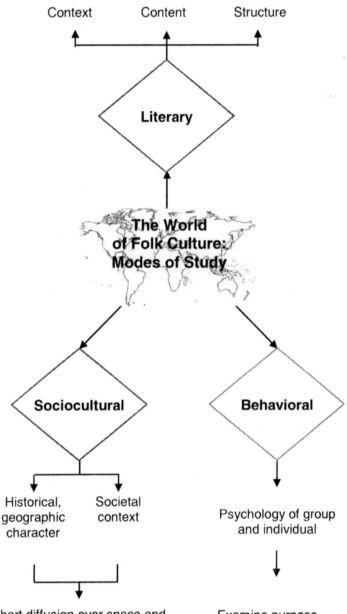

Context   Content   Structure

Literary

The World
of Folk Culture:
Modes of Study

Sociocultural   Behavioral

Historical,   Societal   Psychology of group
geographic   context   and individual
character

Chart diffusion over space and   Examine purpose.
time to show cultural interaction.   Group/individual behavior
Examine role played in culture.   as related to purpose

Figure 1.9.
Author created; world outline image is PD

THE BUILT ENVIRONMENT

Frequently overlooked, the built environment is one of the richest types of primary sources. It consists of the human-made world that we meet every day, from buildings to bridges, stadiums, canals, and roads. As the name suggests, the built environment encompasses all aspects of building from planning to construction. It includes usage and gauging impact. Land use, settlement patterns, community planning, and place names are included in this category.

Building a structure acts like a stone thrown in a pool of still water, creating a ripple effect that can transform a place. No matter if it is a single structure, a revitalization of an existing area, or the creation of a new community, the process involves changing the natural environment to accommodate the structure or community. The construction of a new building creates an equally new footprint that may require new or adapted infrastructure.

As is true of new additions generally, it can change the character of the space and the surrounding community. The actual construction stimulates many aspects of a society. In addition to the building industry, construction can trigger a rise in the production and the employment in such areas as banking, insurance, law, extractive industries, manufacturing, retail, transportation, communication, and government. Its reach can extend far beyond the local community.

After the structure is built, surges can occur in any business activity connected to its maintenance and use. Every building changes the cultural, economic, social, and possibly business activities of the surrounding area. It may even alter the demographics of the area.

The ripple effect is multiplied greatly when an existing area is revitalized. Many cities have sought to revive declining areas with new parks, stadiums, hotels, and convention centers. The rationale is that these venues can help stimulate other commercial, entertainment, and possibly residential growth.

The development of a new community typically involves the total reconstruction of an area, possibly converting farmland into a residential subdivision or a shopping mall, sports stadium, airport, or industrial center. In some cases, urban industrial or declining areas are redeveloped. Development can include planning streets, setting up the infrastructure, and building various structures to serve residential, commercial, and possibly industrial or other purposes. All aspects of community development become part of the study of the built environment.

Place and building names also are important aspects of the built environment. In many U.S. areas, Native American names help identify original inhabitants and may reflect cultural interactions in the meeting of peoples. Public building and street names often honor important individuals. Similarly, when a building is named after a person, it can memorialize a famous individual. Names also identify the builders, the owner, and sometimes, the past or present principal occupants, usually companies or organizations. In other cases, the building's function provides the name. In every instance, the name provides valuable information about the structure and possibly the area.

In one sense, studying an aspect of the built environment is like conducting a microstudy of the development of a society.

The first step in studying the built environment is to establish the provenance of the structure. It involves identifying the architect and/or developer, when it was planned and built, why it was built, and possibly the cost of construction.

Two other perspectives are form and function. Form refers to the look of the structure. It involves examining the type of building, its size, the layout, any materials used in construction, architectural style, technology, and how the structure fits in the surrounding area. As the name suggests, function stresses use, but use can change over time. Technological development can also affect a structure's function. Identifying tenants supplies a wealth of information about a building.

Another focus of studying the built environment is impact. As described above, construction acts as a stimulus. It can have an economic, political, social, or cultural impact on the area. A structure can stimulate an area's revival, acting as an anchor for revitalization. In addition, many structures have historical significance.

Studying the built environment as a primary source reinforces the fact that the everyday, outside world offers unique experiences that bring learning to life.

Teaching the built environment often combines learning outside and inside the classroom. Something as simple as a walk around a school neighborhood, a walking tour of a downtown area, or even a field trip to a shopping mall allows teachers to have students experience the primary source by touching the building or walking across the bridge, perhaps smelling the various aromas—good and bad—in the air, hearing the sounds of everyday life. The sensory experience places students at the site of the topic of study. They become active participants in the life and times of the built environment.

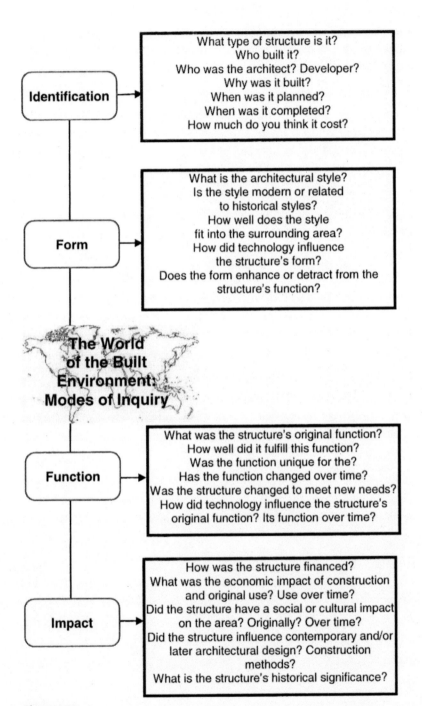

Identification
What type of structure is it?
Who built it?
Who was the architect? Developer?
Why was it built?
When was it planned?
When was it completed?
How much do you think it cost?

Form
What is the architectural style?
Is the style modern or related
to historical styles?
How well does the style
fit into the surrounding area?
How did technology influence
the structure's form?
Does the form enhance or detract from the
structure's function?

The World
of the Built
Environment:
Modes of Inquiry

Function
What was the structure's original function?
How well did it fulfill this function?
Was the function unique for the?
Has the function changed over time?
Was the structure changed to meet new needs?
How did technology influence the structure's
original function? Its function over time?

Impact
How was the structure financed?
What was the economic impact of construction
and original use? Use over time?
Did the structure have a social or cultural impact
on the area? Originally? Over time?
Did the structure influence contemporary and/or
later architectural design? Construction
methods?
What is the structure's historical significance?

Figure 1.10.
Author created; world outline image is PD

MATERIAL CULTURE

Material culture encompasses a wide variety of physical artifacts, virtually all
the objects made by humans for diverse uses. Tools and machines, weapons,
toys and games, clothing, coins and paper money, decorations, utensils, furniture, cell phones and computers, radio and television sets, and containers are
just some of the wide variety of material culture primary sources.

Thanks to the current media vogue with forensics, we have become more
familiar with the value of examining various material culture objects. On
commercial television shows, the context typically is a crime with the objects serving as evidence. Police officers and crime scene investigators (CSI)
scrutinize objects and put them through various tests. The results often tell
detailed stories about the object and its connection to the crime. Other programs use similar techniques to verify authenticity, to ensure the object under
question is genuine. In the process, aspects of the object's manufacture, use,
and impact are explored. All of these programs demonstrate that even the
most mundane artifact can provide great insight and information. The caveat
is that as is true of all primary sources, material culture artifacts tell incomplete and subjective stories.

As the above indicates, the term *material culture* takes in a massive array
of items related to all aspects of the human experience. In fact, much of the
study of archaeology is concerned with the remains of material culture to
access information and gain insight into past cultures. Not only do material
culture artifacts tell us much about a specific people, they also provide potent
evidence for patterns of distribution that can indicate what objects were valued by different peoples.

In many cases, material culture remains are the best or, perhaps, the
only evidence. In *Europe Between the Oceans*, archaeologist Barry Cunliffe traces the distribution of axes made from jadeite in the Alpine area
of the Italian Piedmont and Liguria throughout Europe from southern Italy
to Scotland between 4700 to 3800 BCE. The spread of the axes and the
different types of axes found in various places provide evidence of long-
distance exchange routes, the popularity of the axes among diverse peoples,
and their various uses. For some people, a certain type of jadeite axe was
considered a symbol of status and was likely given as a prestige gift.[27] A
contemporary example could be the spread of certain clothing styles, such
as blue jeans or T-shirts, or technology, such as iPhones or Androids. In all
cases, the objects tell us much about the state of technology, personal tastes,
cultural influence, and trade networks.

Tools are particularly valuable artifacts. A tool can be studied to identify
manufacturing techniques and to gauge the state of technology. It can be

examined to identify work routines. Tools also can be used to explore basic
tenets of a culture or to show how people have interacted with each other and
with the environment. By juxtaposing tools from different societies, students
gain insight not only into the societies, but they also can compare and contrast
these societies.

Take the use of the plow, the hoe, and the stick as a farming implement.
In Europe and in most of the Americas after colonization, the plow drawn
by a draft animal was used to prepare the land for planting. Since forest had
covered much of the land in Europe and in eastern North America, deforesta-
tion was practiced to clear it for planting. A plow was needed to penetrate
the tough soil. Another important factor was that land was used for pasture,
allowing the keeping of draft animals.[28]

According to historian John King Fairbank, historically, Chinese agri-
culture developed differently. Much of the land is covered by loess, a fine,
loosely packed, and mineral-rich soil that is created by wind and glaciers that
grind rocks into a fine powder. Waterways also distribute loess soil in flood-
plains. Loess is easily broken up for farming, making the hoe a likely tool.

In addition, most of the land was devoted to planting crops. Pasture was not
available for draft animals in some areas.

Fairbank also claims that China's large population influenced the reliance
on human labor. The cultivation of rice in the southern regions provided a
much larger source of food than did wheat in Europe or North America, but
it also required substantial manual labor to produce.[29]

A different system of tilling the land arose in some arid regions of Africa and the western United States. In these regions, the topsoil is fragile. It
generally is shallow and friable, meaning it is easily disrupted. To maintain
the topsoil, indigenous people tilled the soil by poking a hole in the ground
with a stick and hand planting the seeds. In this way, the topsoil experienced
minimal disturbance.[30]

The plow, the hoe, and the stick can serve as points of departure for the study
of different cultures. These tools also provide a way to characterize the cultures,
to evaluate the impact of geography on their development, and to compare
them. By focusing on an everyday item, history gains relevance, making a
potentially difficult topic easier to study and to understand. In the process, the
value of material culture artifacts as primary sources is reinforced.

In some ways, nothing brings a student closer to history than examining
or using a material culture artifact. Unfortunately, they are often difficult to
obtain, meaning drawings and photos may be a lesser substitute.

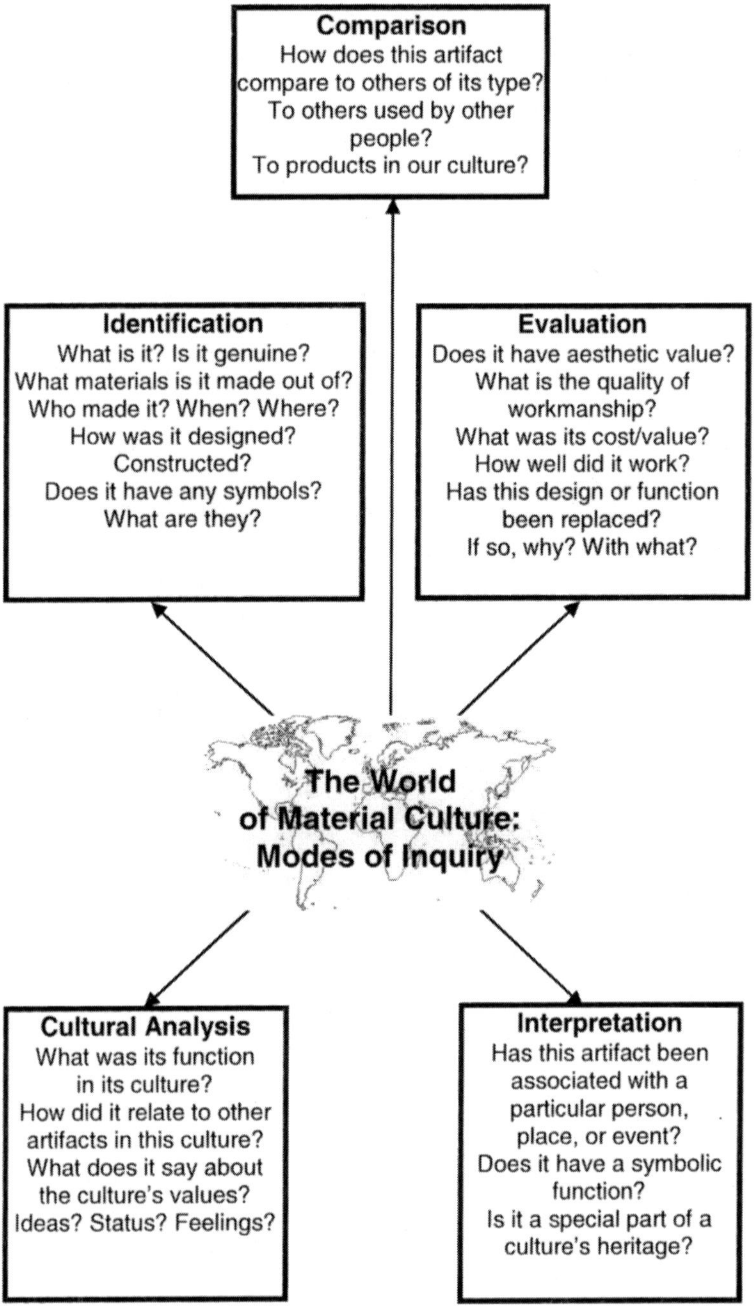

Comparison
How does this artifact compare to others of its type? To others used by other people? To products in our culture?

Identification
What is it? Is it genuine? What materials is it made out of? Who made it? When? Where? How was it designed? Constructed? Does it have any symbols? What are they?

Evaluation
Does it have aesthetic value? What is the quality of workmanship? What was its cost/value? How well did it work? Has this design or function been replaced? If so, why? With what?

The World
of Material Culture:
Modes of Inquiry

Cultural Analysis
What was its function in its culture? How did it relate to other artifacts in this culture? What does it say about the culture's values? Ideas? Status? Feelings?

Interpretation
Has this artifact been associated with a particular person, place, or event? Does it have a symbolic function? Is it a special part of a culture's heritage?

Figure 1.11.
Author created; world outline image is PD

THE NATURAL ENVIRONMENT

An inescapable but frequently overlooked primary source is the natural environment. The influence of landforms, waterways, vegetation, and weather on historical events is often noted, but their study as a primary source document is seldom considered. In some cases, as with weather, it can be difficult, risky, or impossible. Nonetheless, aspects of the natural environment can be valuable primary sources that offer good opportunities for teaching and learning.

The options open for studying the natural environment as a primary source are the same as for the built environment or material culture. You can use visuals (still or motion) or possibly print documents. Best of all, in many cases, you can explore the real thing. One major distinction with the natural environment is that the real thing as it exists at the time of your visit may be quite different than it was at the time being studied. A combination of contemporary accounts and a site visit work best, as they allow students to see the river, lake, mountain, and others as it was and then experience it as it is today.

Visiting the place provides unique opportunities for sensory study beyond sight. A major distinction exists between looking at a picture and actually being there. Students can walk in the shoes of the historical actors. They can smell, feel, hear, and touch the "document." While at the site or afterward, they can make inferences about the experiences, the thoughts, and the feelings of those historical actors.

Since site visits are impossible in most scenarios, visual documents are recommended. Pictures offer a realistic image and leave less to the imagination. Reading a print description requires students to translate the words into their own pictures. Their visions may be very different from the real thing.

Print descriptions work best when they supplement visuals to provide students with more information. For example, in the study of the Civil War, photos and possibly sketches of battlefields can show the terrain, the plant life, and other characteristics that played a role in their outcome. A photograph of Little Round Top at Gettysburg provides insight into how the Union army used the natural environment for defensive purposes.[31] A print account that describes Little Round Top and the action that occurred there adds important information.

Similarly, in world history, students can study the impact of natural disasters by viewing a YouTube video of the 2011 tsunami in Japan that provides a chilling look at that disaster as it happened. They can also read survivor accounts. In early grades in which community is the subject, it may be possible to visit a physical feature of importance to the community.

When using visual imagery, an important first step is establishing provenance to make sure what is depicted is actually the desired place and feature.

The time frame also must be defined. If the visual is from a date later or, perhaps, earlier than the time of the event or place being studied, make that fact clear to students. If the visual was created during a different season or when the weather was different from that occurring at the time of the event, that information also must be taken into account. The same is true regarding the time of day of the actual event versus the time of day of the creation of the visual. In addition, care should be taken to ensure that the natural environment, itself, is the focus of examination as a document.

Whether using a contemporary visual or visiting a site to study the past, the present environment or feature can be compared with what existed in the past to show change over time. Students can examine how the natural environment influenced an event. They also can assess how natural or human action altered the natural environment.

Whatever the scenario, omitting study of the natural environment as a primary source document can mean a missed opportunity for student learning.

NOTES

1. A portion of Jefferson's handwritten Declaration of Independence can be viewed in the Thomas Jefferson Papers collection of the Library of Congress website, http://memory.loc.gov/master/mss/mtj/mtj1/001/0800/0883.jpg.

2. Peter Burke, *Eyewitnessing: The Uses of Images as Historical Evidence* (Ithaca, NY: Cornell University Press, 2001), 9–10, 13–15.

3. Barbara Cruz and Stephen Thornton, "Visualizing Social Studies Literacy: Teaching Content and Skills to English Language Learners," *Social Studies Research & Practice*, 7 (2012): 1–15.

4. Jerry Brotton, *A History of the World in 12 Maps* (New York: Viking, 2012), 84; Gerald Danzer, *World History: An Atlas and Study Guide* (Upper Saddle River, NJ: Prentice Hall, 1998), 26–27.

5. J. B. Harley, "Texts and Contexts in the Interpretations of Early Maps," in *From Sea Charts to Satellite Images: Interpreting North American History through Maps*, ed. David Buisseret (Chicago: University of Chicago Press, 1990), 3–13.

6. Brotton, *A History of the World in 12 Maps*, 218–59, examines the history and impact of the Mercator map.

7. Ibid., 57–58.

8. Ibid., 146–85.

9. Lewis Hine, "Social Photography," in *Classic Essays on Photography*, ed. Alan Trachtenberg (New Haven, CT: Leete's Island Books, 1980), 111. The Hine article was originally published in 1909.

10. Mark Newman, "What Do You See? Exploring the Nature of Photographs as Educational Resources," *Teaching and Learning with Primary Sources*, 1 (2009), accessed January 26, 2014, http://tpsfed.org/TPSJ.htm.

11. Peter Burian and Robert Caputo, *National Geographic Photography Field Guide* (Washington, DC: National Geographic, 2001), 24–26.

12. Samuel Thomas, "Teaching America's GAPE (or any other period) with Political Cartoons: A Systematic Approach to Primary Source Analysis," *The History Teacher*, 37 (2004): 426–7; Michael McCarthy, "Political Cartoons in the History Classroom," *The History Teacher*, 11 (1977): 32–34.

13. David Robinson, *From Peep Show to Palace* (New York: Columbia University Press, 1997), offers a concise history of early cinema.

14. Michael Tierno, *Aristotle's Poetics for Screenwriters: Storytelling Secrets from the Greatest Mind in Western Civilization* (New York: Hyperion, 2002).

15. Adam Woelders, "Using Film to Conduct Historical Inquiry with Middle School Students," *The History Teacher*, 40 (2007): 336–70, explores the issues, promises, and strategies of using film in the classroom.

16. Burke suggests that painters are social historians whose work records aspects of everyday life. Burke, *Eyewitnessing*, 103.

17. Gail Husch, "George Caleb Bingham's *The Country Election*: Whig Tribute to the Will of the People," *American Art Journal*, 19 (1987): 4–22.

18. William Bascom, "Four Functions of Folklore," *Journal of American Folklore*, 67 (1954): 333–49.

19. George Foster, "What Is Folk Culture?" *American Anthropologist*, 55 (1953): 159–73.

20. Kwesi Yankah, "Proverb Rhetoric and African Judicial Processes: The Untold Story," *Journal of American Folklore*, 99 (1986): 280–303.

21. David Evans, *Big Road Blues: Tradition and Creativity in the Folk Blues* (Berkeley: University of California Press, 1982), offers an insightful account of how blues songs are constructed and performed.

22. Albert Lord, *The Singer of Tales* (Cambridge: Harvard University Press, 1981), is the classic study.

23. C. A. Weslager, *The Log Cabin in America: From Pioneer Days to the Present* (New Brunswick, NJ: Rutgers University Press, 1969).

24. An excellent examination of the Clovis point and Clovis culture is in Steven Mithen, *After the Ice: A Global Human History, 20,000–5,000 BC* (Cambridge: Harvard University Press, 2003), 212–4, 246–57.

25. Alfred Crosby, *Ecological Imperialism: The Biological Expansion of Europe, 900–1900* (New York: Cambridge University Press, 1986), 145–217, explores the exchange of plants, animals, and disease. See also Jared Diamond, *Guns, Germs, and Steel: The Fates of Human Societies* (New York: W. W. Norton & Company, 1998).

26. A good source for Native American creation stories featuring coyote is Richard Erdoes and Alfonso Ortiz, compilers and editors, *American Indian Myths and Legends* (New York: Pantheon, 1985), 1–24.

27. Barry Cunliffe, *Europe between the Oceans, 9000 BC–AD 1000* (New Haven: CT: Yale University Press, 2008), 152.

28. Ibid., 96–106, examines the first farmers in Europe.

29. John K. Fairbank, Edwin O. Reischauer, and Albert M. Craig, *East Asia: Tradition and Transformation*, revised edition (Cambridge: Harvard University Press, 1989), 18.

30. Roger Blench, "African Agricultural Tools: Implications of Synchronic Ethnography for Agrarian History" (paper presented, fifth International Workshop for African Archaeology, July 1–4, 2006, revised 2007). Accessed January 27, 2014 at Academia.edu, http://www.academia.edu/2326505/African_agricultural_tools_impli cations_of_synchronic_ethnography_for_agrarian_history.

31. Pictures of Little Round Top are available on the Library of Congress website at http://www.loc.gov/pictures/search/?q=little+round+top&st=gallery, accessed January 26, 2014.

Part Two

How Can Primary Sources
Be Used in the Classroom?

Primary sources are versatile and valuable educational resources. The diversity of types and the varied lengths enable them to fit into almost any learning experience. The combination of the wide array of sources available and the specific content of each primary source document provides teachers with numerous options for classroom use.

Primary sources also add value in the classroom. Since they are the real thing, so to speak, primary sources bring students closer to the people, places, and times being studied. And their use integrates learning content with skills development.

To meet their full potential as an educational resource, primary source documents need to be situated within a viable context that integrates their classroom use on a regular basis over time. A structure is needed to create a pattern of teaching and learning that extends across the entire school year. That structure integrates primary sources into the larger flow of learning so they become part of the classroom routine. The old adage that practice makes perfect applies. Working with primary source documents over time increases student familiarity and proficiency.[1]

Inquiry-based learning (IBL) supplies a viable context for primary source use. Before looking into IBL, perhaps some basic questions need answering. What is inquiry-based learning? Why should teachers use it?

At the most basic level, inquiry-based learning is a method that structures student learning around a cycle of asking questions and seeking answers to understand a topic of study.[2] The idea is for students to use what the C3 Framework for State Social Studies Standards calls compelling questions to focus their study of a topic. Supporting questions are more focused queries that offer a way to inquire into source documents to build a database of information that can be used to answer the compelling question.

Why use inquiry-based learning? There are several reasons. IBL provides teachers with a teaching and learning structure that actively engages students in their learning. By design, the question-and-answer cycle sets up a well-organized, smooth flow of learning with a defined beginning, middle, and end. The process also offers a flexible, versatile method that has students regularly practice skills and work with content multiple times to improve their competency.

IBL also makes students responsible for their learning. As students become more adept at the inquiry method, teacher presence diminishes. They pursue their studies with more independence and confidence. Their skills improve, and they better understand the content.[3]

Not surprisingly, for several decades, history and social studies teachers have been asked to use disciplinary inquiry methods in their classrooms.[4] Besides the improvement in skills and content knowledge, scholars claim it teaches students how history and related social studies disciplines work. In the process, students practice important disciplinary habits of mind.

Recent developments have intensified the need for inquiry-based learning. Common Core literacy standards for social studies require developing skills connected to an inquiry method, and the C3 Framework for State Social Studies Standards is based on an inquiry arc model of learning.

As indicated above, IBL has some impressive upsides. It also has some downsides. Recent studies suggest that inquiry-based learning is not well understood by history and social studies educators.[5] In part, the lack of understanding may be due to the limited studies and curricular models in history and social studies. Even a cursory search of the literature on IBL shows that research on science predominates. The scholarly stress on science is not surprising since it has a long tradition of inquiry that has fostered many models.

History and social studies teachers usually have to construct their own inquiry-based learning models that address the reality that students often find it difficult to evaluate meaning from varied texts.[6] Examining primary source documents involves much more than just identifying content. Establishing provenance, identifying the purpose and message, evaluating accuracy and bias, determining what is missing, and analyzing form and style are part of the inquiry investigation.

Another aspect concerns the researcher. All of us approach a topic, a question, a text with prior knowledge and preconceived notions that can influence our study. For inquiry to work, teacher and student need to be aware of all these things.

In addition, pedagogically, IBL can be a literal sea change of practice for teacher and student. Barton and Levstik suggested that some teachers knowledgeable about IBL did not necessarily use it in the classroom. Because inquiry-based learning centers on the student and in-depth studies, it went against the teachers' perception that their major tasks were to control student behavior and cover content.[7]

In IBL, the teacher as leader and presenter is replaced increasingly over time by the teacher acting as facilitator. Preparation before class increases greatly, while teacher tasks in the classroom likely diminish over time. In essence, inquiry slowly but surely takes control of learning away from the teacher, placing it on the student. Just as teachers may have difficultly adapting to the changes IBL requires, students may encounter similar problems if they are used to a routine that stresses certain behavior and surveying content.

Content learning also changes as inquiry focuses attention on certain topics and themes. Coverage becomes less important than deeper exploration. What content students learn is prioritized, but they also need a strong overview of what they are studying. Balancing the mix of gaining the larger people, place, and time context with the in-depth investigation requires careful planning and implementation.

The primary source documents raise another potential barrier. A dilemma many teachers face is that students are unable to read an otherwise excellent primary source. The grammar, spelling, and vocabulary of a document may be archaic or above grade level. Another issue is the quality of the document's resolution and clarity. Handwritten documents can be blurry, or the writing itself may be difficult to make out. Visuals, especially maps, can lose resolution as they move from computer screen or original to photocopy.

Given the balance of up and down sides, teaching and learning with IBL can be an intrepid adventure. It also can be rewarding, because, in most cases, the obstacles can be overcome. If IBL represents a major change for teachers and students, both need to be aware that a learning curve exists.[8]

When guided by clearly stated rules of behavior, actively engaged students are less likely to create discipline problems. The class time goes by faster, leaving few lulls in the action that can spawn misbehavior.[9] Obviously, each teacher needs to monitor his or her classroom situation and apply IBL methods accordingly.

Three important points are: first, keep everything simple and basic. Second, it is possible to implement inquiry methods over time, perhaps, starting with examining primary sources and moving on to a fuller inquiry as students become more competent. Third, until students demonstrate mastery, much of the inquiry method can feature heavy scaffolding. Teacher release and control become less problematic as both teacher and student become more familiar with the routine and more expert at inquiry-based learning.

The big-picture model described below addresses many concerns over the release of control and the combining of the survey overview with the more focused investigation. The all-learner curriculum discussed below also provides strategies to help all students succeed within an IBL environment.

The issues of document language and clarity can be addressed in various ways. Providing students with a glossary of terms can ease vocabulary difficulties. Another option is to have students view the original so they can see what it looks like, but provide a rewritten version at the appropriate reading level. Students get the flavor of the original but access the document through a version they can read.

With visuals, teachers can provide students with more than one version of the image. The best resolution tends to be on the computer screen. When computers are not available for every student, the teacher can project the image for general viewing and provide students with a photocopy for individual reference.

The following pages provide a description of classroom-tested curricular materials, including the big-picture inquiry model and a collection of primary-source-based learning exercises. Each exercise is prefaced by an introductory description and, where necessary, pertinent information on the primary source documents.

The big-picture model and the exercises supply examples of classroom procedures. While they might be used as is, to meet local conditions adaptations will be necessary. The exercises span the three major social studies content areas: U.S. history, world history, and community. Although not all of the numerous possibilities are shown, the examples offer a taste of the wide range of the potential primary source exercises. The section ends with an all-learner curriculum developed to accommodate second-language learners and students with special needs.

THE BIG-PICTURE INQUIRY-BASED LEARNING METHOD

The big-picture inquiry-based learning method was developed to help students manage information so they could make sense of the heavy content in a world history course.[10] It also was used in U.S. history courses, but it has general applicability. The model has been revised over time to the version described below.

As the name suggests, the goal is for students to gain a big-picture understanding of a topic of study. The rationale was that if students could manage all the content studied about a history topic and compose a one-sentence thesis to answer the compelling question (to use C3 Framework language) that guided their inquiry, they could show what they had learned. Equally important, they had to develop evidence to support the thesis, presenting their findings in writing or some other format.

While content provides the structure for learning, the big-picture model follows a skills-based organization. It has three related phases that has students practice similar skills in different scenarios. The first phase opens the inquiry, acting as an abbreviated version of the inquiry model. Students study a primary source, using an adapted close-reading method that has them identify content, establish the provenance of the source, and then pose questions to focus the study of the topic.

Posing questions is often a difficult task. For compelling questions, an open-ended format works best, as it leaves the answer open to interpretation. Supporting questions are more focused. They can be open-ended or direct. Compelling questions are discussed here.

A good, compelling question has three parts: the topic, the interrogative (generally at a high skill level), and the focus of the inquiry. The topic typically is the name of the unit or a variation of the name. The interrogative identifies the task, most often answering the question why, or perhaps combining how and why. The focus is generally a theme or subtopic. The focus can act as examples to be studied to answer the question.

For example, studying early civilizations is a staple of many world history courses. A viable, compelling question could be: Why did the first civilizations arise in river valleys? Since studying first civilizations appears early in the school year, this question is quite specific. If students are more expert in IBL, the question could be stated as: Why did the first civilizations arise when and where they did?

We will explore the first query on emerging river valleys. The topic is first civilizations. The interrogative asks students to evaluate why they arose where they did. The focus is river valleys, identifying potential in-depth studies in Mesopotamia, Egypt, the Indus River Valley civilization, and possibly the Wei River Valley in China. The topic requires students to get an overview of the era during which the civilizations arose so they have a people, space, and time context to their studies. It also has them identify first civilizations as the priority.

Later in the school year, the compelling question can be less explicit but still needs the three components. Depending upon student competency, a compelling question to use in the study of the Industrial Revolution may or may not provide more leeway. A clearly defined question could be: How and why did the Industrial Revolution originate when and where it did? A more open-ended query might be: Why or why not was the Industrial Revolution revolutionary? In both cases, the topic is the Industrial Revolution. The first query has two interrogatives: how and why. So does the second, as it asks students to select why or why not.

The example for the first question identifies the origin of the Industrial Revolution as the example. It requires students to have learned that it originated in Great Britain, but it also indicates that the experience of other nations needs to be studied to provide an important time and place context. The example for the second question is the revolutionary character or lack thereof in industrialization. It, too, requires studying various examples.

By the time of the Industrial Revolution and other later units, it might also be possible for students to pose their own compelling question based on the initial primary source analysis. The question can be revised as needed, after exploring the people, space, and time context described in the next paragraph.

Phase two expands the investigation, initiating the question-and-answer cycle. First, students develop the people, space, and time context to get a larger picture of the topic. Map work, creating timelines or chronologies, and writing biographies are typical exercises. Depending upon student ability, either the teacher or the students can choose specific subtopics for in-depth study. A quiz following the overview assesses how well students know the larger picture.

Next, they examine primary and secondary source texts to compile a database and to answer supporting questions as well as to pose new queries as needed. Following the examination of sources, the database is managed to prioritize and to categorize information. Guided by the questions and answers, duplicative and irrelevant data are eliminated. The objective is to organize the information into a small number of categories. Typically three is the magic number, but certainly no more than five.

The last step is to create the answer. The one-sentence thesis is developed. Evidence is marshaled to support the thesis. The answer is then developed to present the findings.

It is important that students understand how to construct the thesis statement. Just as posing questions should follow a certain formula, so the same is true of developing the thesis statement. Above all else, students must understand that the thesis statement serves two purposes. Most important, it directly and succinctly answers the compelling question. But it also is constructed to identify the examples that will be used to support that answer.

As such, the thesis has three components. First, the topic needs to be stated so the context is clear. Second, the answer is succinctly expressed. Third, major aspects of the topic are identified that will be used as examples to defend the thesis.

Though varying methods exist to craft a thesis, using the key-words strategy often helps focus students on the task. The key-word approach uses the unit topic and draws upon the terms from the various categories to guide the writing of the thesis statement. An important point is that there is not one correct thesis statement. Various explanations are possible in any inquiry scenario. How correct a thesis statement is depends upon how relevant it is to the topic, how well it answers the question, and both the effectiveness of the argument and the evidence used to support that argument.

Using the river valley unit as an example, let us assume that favorable conditions, unfavorable conditions, and society characteristics were information categories. A potential thesis statement is: The first civilizations arose in river valleys because the combination of favorable and unfavorable conditions in Mesopotamia, Egypt, and the Indus River Valley influenced the development of societies complex enough to be called civilizations.

Examining the thesis statement shows that the topic is stated at the beginning of the statement. The answer and the examples are integrally related. The thesis is that the combination of favorable and unfavorable conditions in the river valleys stimulated the development of societies complex and long-lived enough to be called civilizations. The examples are three civilizations studied.

After developing the thesis, students use information from the categories to identify examples to provide support. The findings can be presented in an essay, orally, or using technology.

Since the big-picture model will be a new way of teaching and learning, it is best to proceed slowly and cautiously. The bottom line for any inquiry model is that students need to succeed for it to work. The discussion that follows offers ideas, but teachers should adapt the process to meet the need of their students.

In the initial unit or units, whole-class modeling helps familiarize students with the process and provides teachers with the means to evaluate student proficiency and progress. The initial inquiry into a primary source can serve as a diagnostic to evaluate student skills so that teachers can adjust what follows as needed.

Whole class and group work dominate the activities. Depending upon skill level and experience with primary source documents, students can work as a whole class or in groups to explore sources. Since it is important that each student has the same database, whole-class discussion is needed to share the people, space, and time context as well as the results of the primary and secondary source analysis.

As noted above, a good time for a quiz is after students complete the various tasks related to the larger context. Unless students have good working knowledge of the people, the places, and the time frame of the unit, it might be difficult for them to pursue in-depth studies effectively.

Crafting the thesis statement is generally a whole-class exercise. An interesting twist is to have the class develop the thesis statement and then give students the option of defending or refuting that statement. The development of the essay, the oral presentation, or the technology product is best done individually, though group work can be used for oral or technology presentations.

The last point concerns content learning and skills development. In the big-picture model, students work with content several times in differing contexts from primary source analysis, to working with maps, timelines, and biographies, to organizing information and synthesizing it into a thesis statement, to developing and presenting evidence to support the thesis.

Throughout the process, they practice a similar skills set of reading, critical thinking, managing information, and decision making. Moving toward the thesis statement, the skills are practiced to create a database and the thesis. To support the thesis, similar skills are practiced in the opposite direction to mine the database for specific, pertinent information.

Virtually all of the Common Core literacy skills are used in the big-picture model. The four dimensions of the C3 Framework Inquiry Arc are also embedded into this model.[11]

CLASSROOM EXERCISES

This section provides a variety of classroom-tested exercises to fit different scenarios. The examples span the three major history and social studies content areas: world history, U.S. history, and community. They feature a number of different types of primary sources.

While the exercises can be used as is, it is more likely they will need to be adapted to meet local classroom conditions. If feasible, the type of primary source and the number of documents used can be adjusted. The activity itself can be revised.

The Common Core literacy standards the exercise meets are listed. Standards from the C3 Framework for State Social Studies Standards are not listed because these are purportedly guides for states rather than mandated standards. The classroom exercises fit into the following categories:

1. Exploring the Nature of Primary Sources

   For students to use primary sources effectively as learning resources, they must understand their subjective, incomplete nature. The examples can easily be integrated into units of study.

Big Picture Inquiry-Based Learning Method

Step One: Introduce Topic and Method	Primary source document inquiry: 1. Introduce topic. 2. Model inquiry method. 3. Pose compelling and supporting questions.	1. Identify information and vocabulary. 2. Identify potential sub-topics and concepts. 3. Review information to pose compelling and supporting questions.
Step Two: Explore Topic and Practice Method	Primary and secondary sources, including textbook inquiry into topic and sub-topics: 1. Build database of information. 2. Define vocabulary 3. Answer supporting questions and pose new queries as needed.	1. Read sources using supporting questions as guide to identify pertinent ideas and information. 2. Compare new and existing data to assess perspective and facts. 3. Use comparison results to tentatively answer supporting questions, pose new queries if needed.
Step Three: Managing Data	Analysis of database: 1. Organize information. 2. Answer supporting questions. 3. Develop evidence to support answers.	1. Review database to eliminate repetition 2. Select pertinent data related to sub-topics/supporting questions. 3. Categorize data by sub-topic/supporting questions.
Step Four: Synthesis	Present findings: 1. Develop thesis to answer compelling question. 2. Create thesis and argument in required format. 3. Present findings.	1. Review answers and data. 2. Synthesize review into one-sentence thesis answering compelling question. 3. Identify three major points and supporting data from answers to support thesis.

Figure 2.1.
Author created

2. Opening or Closing a Unit

   These activities are primarily geared to serve as unit openers, the initial phase of the big-picture model. But they can be adapted for use to close a unit.

   In addition, the two types of document-based question (DBQ) formats are discussed: inquiry units and assessment. No examples are provided since these tend to be specific to the classroom and the unit.

WHICH WAY IS UP?

Maps are familiar classroom resources. While they are versatile documents open to varied uses, most often, students use maps to identify where the topic of study and relevant places are located. The use of maps builds on the idea that mapping behavior, "the thinking and action involved in reading, making, and using map-like models," is a universal cultural trait that we acquire as young children.[12]

Maps provide a spatial construct that allows us to make sense of ourselves in relation to the world. At the most basic instructional level, maps tell us "where" what is being studied, and, perhaps, where we are located in relation to the topic of study. Locating the places being studied and comparing those locations to where we are provides us with a sense of space.

Or does it? Maps project a certain view of the world. Students using a map for any classroom task generally see a uniform picture of the planet. Often, the assumption is that the map is an accurate and faithful representation of the world, that what is depicted is trustworthy. That assumption is false.

Maps are cultural texts, and they have the same nature as all primary sources: they are subjective and incomplete. While technology and recent projections have helped eliminate some of the distortions of earlier map formats, orientation remains an issue.

The maps we see inside and outside the classroom follow the same orientation. North is up. The pervasiveness of that orientation can create the impression that, indeed, the earth is situated in the universe so that north is up.

The issue of orientation needs explanation. The northern orientation has not always predominated in mapping. If the entire history of maps is considered, the overwhelming preeminence of north is a recent development of the last five hundred years. Historically, maps have been created with other directions to the top. A good way to impress upon students that maps specifically and primary sources generally are subjective texts is to explore the various orientations. In addition, these orientations offer valuable insight into the cultures that created the maps.

In the past, each of the cardinal directions had a symbolic meaning assigned by the culture creating the map that influenced how it was oriented. In Europe, the Middle East, and Asia, religion, culture, and politics determined which direction was placed at the top of a map. For reference purposes, the favored orientations of various groups and cultures are as follows:

- Based on the idea that east was the location of paradise, early Christians and the Roman Catholic Church prior to 1492 favored an eastern orientation.
- North was the most popular orientation. It was favored by the Chinese because the emperor's palace and throne as well as the entrance to the emperor's tomb faced south, meaning worshippers had to face north. Because Shinto altars faced south, entering them meant going north, so Japanese maps used north. The Persian-Mesopotamian cartographic tradition considered the pole star as a source of light, healing, and instruction. Gnostic/Dualist Christian groups adopted that tradition. In turn, the Protestant church drew on Gnostic/Dualist influence and used north to show opposition to the Roman Catholic Church. Lastly, north was up on European maps after the recovery of Ptolemy's works. Mercator used north in his influential map.
- South was at the top of Muslim maps in part because early conquests were to the north, meaning Mecca was south. Islamic maps also may have been influenced by Zoroastrians in Persia who had south as the favored direction.

No cultural tradition placed west at the top since that direction was connected to death and darkness, being the place that the sun set.[13]

The supremacy of the northern orientation began in Europe during the Reformation. But as Gordon states, "In navigating with the compass and in making maps, nautical or otherwise, north has no special advantage over south." Nor does he suggest that it has an advantage over east or west.[14]

Which way is up?, the activity below, has students examine four maps to gain a better understanding of orientation and the various influences on mapmaking. The maps are not reproduced in the book. Instead, URLs and digital IDs are provided in the Notes section so that the reader can access the highest quality images possible.

The first two maps show that the northern orientation does have a long tradition dating back over two thousand years. They include a current reference map that can be taken from any textbook followed by the world map constructed by Byzantine scribes in the late thirteen century based on *Geography* written by Ptolemy in the second century. *Geography* had no maps, but it offered mapmaking instructions that guided the later drawing of maps and served as a standard projection until 1492. Though drawn centuries later, the Ptolemy world map is a prime example of classical Hellenistic cartography.[15]

Next come two maps with different orientations. The al-Idrisi Islamic world map is oriented with south to the top, reflecting religious beliefs.[16] The medieval European Hereford map is oriented with east to the top, reflecting the religious worldview of Europe during that time.[17] If need be, other examples from differing cultures can be used, although these maps are well known and easy to find.

An important point the teacher should stress is that these maps were created on very different materials. The reference map example will likely have been printed on paper or created digitally. Ptolemy's map is a later paper or parchment construction from his *Geography* that was handwritten on papyrus. The Islamic map was originally created on a silver disk. The Hereford map was drawn on vellum made from the hide of an ox.[18]

Though resources on the historical maps are listed in the notes to this section, they need some explanation.

The Ptolemy world map depicts the Hellenistic vision of the known world in the second century CE.[19] Ptolemy lived in Alexandria, Egypt, a center of classical knowledge and learning founded by Alexander the Great. It featured perhaps the world's largest library that contained an estimated five hundred thousand works, representing what Jerry Brotton has called "the collective memory" of the classical world.[20]

Claudius Ptolemy was an astronomer and mathematician. His *Geography* served several purposes. It provided the latitude and longitude of over eight thousand locations in Africa, Asia, and Europe. It explained astronomy's role in geography, offered a detailed mathematical guide for mapmaking, and included a treatise on geography.

The world map drawn from Ptolemy's *Geography* has north to the top. It is plotted mathematically using a graticule, a grid of meridians (north-south lines) and parallels (east-west lines), on which the map is drawn.

Because the Americas and Australasia were unknown to Ptolemy, they are missing from the map, as are most of the Atlantic and all of the Pacific Ocean.

While Africa, Asia, and Europe are easily recognized, there are some important inaccuracies. Africa curls around to join Asia, making the Indian Ocean an inland sea. Parts of northern Europe are shown as a series of islands. South Asia appears as an island off the coast of Asia. The Mediterranean is extended too far west.

The Ptolemy world map does not have the religious connotations of the following two examples. It symbolized the scientific thrust of the Hellenistic world that drew on Greek philosophy and scholarship. Ptolemy's map influenced Gerhard Mercator, helping make north the standard orientation in western cartography.

Muslim scholar Abu Abdallah Muhammad ibn Muhammad ibn Idris, called al-Sharif al-Idrisi, created the next map. He is commonly known as al-Idrisi. In the early 1440s, he was commissioned by King Roger II of Sicily to create a collection of geographical knowledge. After working almost fifteen years on the task, al-Idrisi published the *Entertainment for He Who Longs to Travel the World.*

Drawing upon Greek, Christian, and Islamic traditions, the *Entertainment*, as it is known, included narrative and maps. In preparation for the volume, al-Idrisi created a world map on a silver disk. While that map has been lost, print versions were included in the *Entertainment.*[21]

Although drawing on diverse cultural sources, the al-Idrisi world map does represent a school of contemporary Islamic cartography. At that time, Islamic scholars were well aware of classical Greek and Roman works. Along with various European monasteries, Islamic scholars played a pivotal role in the preservation and later transmission of classical scholarship. The world map is a good example of this cultural synthesis.

Following an Islamic cartographic tradition, the map is oriented to the south. For the exercise described here, that is the key point. The world is round and surrounded by water. Reflecting Ptolemaic influence, al-Idrisi divided the world into seven climate zones. Following Islamic tradition, the world map is centered on Mecca, and the earth's landmass is depicted as a connected whole rather than as divided into continents. Another Ptolemaic influence is curving Africa east, though it does not touch Asia. The far northern regions and much of Europe and Asia are distorted. South Asia is not shown, replaced by a series of islands.

The last map reflects the worldview of medieval Europe. The Hereford map may be the most alien of the maps to be studied. It was produced around 1275 and is an example of a *mappamundi*, literally "map of the world," a cartographic tradition popular in Europe during this period.

The Hereford follows a T-O construction. A ring of water surrounds the landmasses, and the major rivers form a *T*, dividing the continents of Africa, Asia, and Europe. The map is enormous, measuring five feet, two inches by four feet, four inches. Unlike the previous examples, its primary purpose is not to depict the earth or to plot locations. It cannot be used pragmatically to measure distance or to go from here to there.

Mappamundi generally and the Hereford specifically are religious, depicting a Christian-defined world. By the thirteenth century, Europe was close to being Christianized.[22] The *mappamundi* visually celebrated that achievement.

Part of the process of Christianization at that time was replacing the previous classical ideas and beliefs based on science with Christian theology.

Mappamundi were used to promote the idea of pilgrimage and faith in Europe. The Hereford map can be read to tell a tale of the path to salvation. Reflecting prevailing western Christian beliefs, it is oriented with east to the top. Again, that is our major concern. Jerusalem, the pilgrim's destination, is in the center. How the path goes has been interpreted in various ways.

The interpretation here follows the path from the west at the bottom to east at the top. The Pillars of Hercules, a pagan reference, is at the bottom. The journey to salvation starts at the bottom where paganism exists and leads to Jerusalem where conversion and commitment to Christianity occur. Moving east, the tower of Babylon represents temptation. Succumb to temptation and suffer in eternity. Resist temptation and the journey ends at the top, in paradise.

No matter what interpretation is used, in a very graphic way, the Hereford map provided a guide to an acceptable Christian life. It also stresses the predominance of faith and adherence to religious doctrine in medieval Europe.

The following exercise is best done as a whole-class activity, in part because the maps have the clearest resolution when they are projected or viewed on computer screens. Projection also provides a single focal point, facilitating the explanation and reading of the maps. This activity is for middle school or high school. It can be adapted as needed to meet time frames. It is a one-day activity. The exercise meets Common Core literacy standards Key Ideas and Details 1–5, Craft and Structure 1–4, and Integration of Knowledge 1–3.

Topic: Which Way Is Up?

Objectives: By the end of this activity, students will be able to:

1. Read a map for content.
2. Identify orientation as a cultural tradition.
3. Explain why map orientation underscores the idea that maps are subjective by nature.

Procedures:

1. Introduction

   Ask students, "Which way is up?" Most should answer north. Follow up by asking, "Why do you think north is up?" Record the answers. For both queries, prompt students as needed to provide the context of up being applied to the earth and, if needed, lead them to maps as an influence on why they think north is up.

Introduce the activity, explaining that students will study various maps to answer the question, Which way is up?

2. Reading Maps

(Note: Students can be provided with brief introductions to each map, using the descriptions above, or the teacher can provide the context orally. The key point here is examining orientation, though other aspects of the map can be explored. Examining each map should take between five to seven minutes.)

Project a current world map and ask students to identify what direction is up. After they answer north, ask them if any other direction would work, recording their answers and reasoning. No matter what their answers are, the point is that they will begin thinking about map orientation.

Project the Ptolemy world map and introduce its provenance. Also stress that Ptolemy did not provide maps, but rather instructions for drawing them. This map is an example. Point out geographic features such as Africa curling around to meet Asia, that the Indian Ocean is an inland sea, and that the western hemisphere is missing since it was not known to Ptolemy. Ask students the following questions, indicating pertinent map features as needed.

a. What are the vertical and horizontal lines on the maps? Have students refer to the current world map as needed to identify longitude and latitude. Define *graticule*, and explain that Ptolemy mathematically plotted location to identify places.
b. What is the orientation? Which way is up? Students should easily recognize north, but prompt as needed.

Project the al-Idrisi map. Ask students if it looks familiar. Identify its orientation as south to the top, noting it is an Islamic map and follows the Islamic tradition of southern orientation. Explain it was originally created on a huge, silver disk, but that disk was lost. Provide the map's provenance. Note that the map synthesized Islamic, classical Greek and Roman, and Christian schools of cartography.

Rotate the map so it has north to the top, and ask if it is any more familiar. Ask students the following questions, providing information as needed.

a. What is in the center? Identify Mecca if students are unable to do so.
b. What are the horizontal lines across the map? Have you seen anything like these on the other maps? Identify as latitude lines designating climate zones.

c. Do any features look similar to any of the previous maps? Focus student attention on Africa and the Indian Ocean. Students should see a connection to Ptolemy.
   d. Close the discussion by asking students to assess how the influences on the map affected its orientation and projection of the world, leading to the idea of a synthesis that followed Islamic orientation and classical Hellenistic map projections.

Project the Hereford map. Describe the materials used to make the map and provide the provenance, defining *mappamundi* for the students. Project the redrawn Hereford map, and ask students questions as follows, providing help as needed. If need be, provide students with paper copies of the redrawn map for individual reference.

a. What is in the center of the map? What does that tell you about the culture of Europe at the time? Students should identify Jerusalem as the center and religion as the dominant cultural aspect of Europe. Briefly state that Europe was called Christendom at the time.
   b. What is the orientation of the map? Have students plot the direction from Europe to Jerusalem to identify east as up.
   c. If time allows, take students on the journey to salvation using the map as a guide. Ask students what the purpose of the map was. Note that it provided a graphic blueprint to the Christian life and also promoted pilgrimages to the Holy Land.

3. Conclusion

Synthesize the orientations of the various maps, having students identify similarities and differences. Ask students if there are any hard and set rules that determine which way is up on a map.

Query students about what they learned about maps as texts, leading to answers that they are influenced by culture and thus have a specific message to send. Ask students if they can trust what a map tells them without evaluating it. Use their answers to close the exercise by defining maps as subjective and incomplete.

WHAT DID THE DECLARATION OF INDEPENDENCE SAY?

The Declaration of Independence is a founding document of the United States. It also is a seminal primary source in U.S. and often world history and social studies courses. Thirty-four-year-old Thomas Jefferson wrote the Declaration.

On June 7, 1776, the Continental Congress appointed Benjamin Franklin, John Adams, Roger Livingston, Roger Sherman, and Jefferson to a committee charged with drafting an independence statement. Initially, the story goes, Jefferson balked at writing the document, suggesting John Adams should be the author. Adams responded that Jefferson was a much better writer, and the matter was settled. On July 2, 1776, the Continental Congress voted for independence from Great Britain, and its members signed Jefferson's revised draft two days later.[23]

The U.S. Declaration of Independence is a rich, multifaceted document that offers teachers a unique opportunity. Students can explore prevailing political ideas and realities at the time. They can examine a long tradition of using a compact to form a community that dates back to the religious covenants of biblical times and that reached a culmination with Jefferson's statement. They can increase their understanding of the nature of primary sources. And they can view an example of rhetoric that can be used to improve their own writing.

The following exercise uses an adapted close-reading strategy to examine the Declaration from varying perspectives. Depending upon students' skills, it is a one-to-two-day activity. It meets Common Core Reading Standards for Social Studies and History Anchor standards: Key Ideas and Details 1–6 and Craft and Structure 1–4.

Topic: The U.S. Declaration of Independence

Objectives: By the end of this exercise, students will be able to:

1. Evaluate the varied purposes of the U.S. Declaration of Independence.
2. Infer the differing messages diverse historical figures may have received from reading the Declaration.
3. Evaluate the subjective, incomplete nature of the Declaration of Independence.

Procedures:

1. Introduction

   Introduce the Declaration of Independence and have students use prior learning to place it in its historical context.

   Orient students to the exercise, explaining they will be studying the Declaration from several perspectives.

2. Exploring Structure and Content

   As a whole class, read the Declaration paragraph by paragraph to identify the thrust of each paragraph and its important content items.

   Before discussing the content, have students reread the Declaration, using their notes as a guide. Note that the Declaration is a superb example of rhetoric following a classic structure of an introduction, an examination of three examples, and a conclusion. Briefly discuss the value of using the Declaration to improve their essay writing skills.

Discuss its purposes, reasoning, and argument. Query students as to the purpose of the document, having them point out pertinent information in the Declaration to support their answers. An obvious first purpose is to declare independence from Great Britain.

Next, have them review the first and second paragraphs to identify the reasoning behind independence, stressing the need to explain breaking political bonds based on self-evident truths.

Have students review the last paragraph to identify its message; namely, the creation of the United States of America. Query students as to how this paragraph adds another purpose; namely, the founding of the new nation.

If students are familiar with the idea of a social compact, have them apply that idea to the Declaration. Note that the document is one-half of the U.S. social compact, the preamble of the Constitution being the other half. If students are unfamiliar with a social compact, this is a good time to introduce it. Have students relate the purpose of social compacts to earlier documents such as the Mayflower Compact, introducing the tradition of forming communities with agreements that date back to biblical times.

3. Making Inferences

Divide the class into pairs and assign each pair an identity of one of the following as needed: Thomas Jefferson, King George III, Abigail Adams, a Loyalist, a colonist neutral to the dispute with Great Britain, an African slave, the foreign minister of France, the foreign minister of Spain, and an Iroquois.

Have students refer to the Declaration of Independence, and write a brief paragraph inferring what message their historical figure may have received from the document.

Discuss the varied messages, making a list to show their diversity.

1. Thomas Jefferson, patriot: declare independence and form a new nation.
2. King George III: treason by a faction of colonists.
3. Abigail Adams (John Adams's wife): hope for rights for women.
4. Loyalist: treason by a minority of the colonial population, coopting the political debate. Note that roughly one-third of the colonists were loyalists, one-third were patriots, and one-third were neutral.
5. Neutral: coopting of the political debate. The student makes a decision regarding the future for this person who has not necessarily taken a side.
6. African slave: rights and freedom.
7. Foreign Minister of France and Spain: plea for aid against an old enemy.

8. Iroquois: another round in European relations requiring a careful balance of power diplomacy.

3. Conclusion

As a whole class, review the exercise and relate it to both the Declaration of Independence and primary sources generally.

Close the exercise by discussing the subjective, incomplete nature of primary sources and what the implications of that nature are for students using them. Use the varying messages sent by the Declaration, the differing perspectives on these messages, and the incomplete quality of both the content of the document and its purposes.

EUROPEAN IMMIGRANTS ARRIVING IN THE UNITED STATES, EARLY 1900s

At the turn of the twentieth century, the United States experienced a huge influx of immigrants from all parts of the world, but mostly from Europe. New technological advances in photography and the recent invention of motion pictures contributed to amassing a rich, visual record of immigration. The photographs used in this exercise and others related to immigration at the turn of the twentieth century are easily accessed on the Library of Congress (www.loc.gov) website by using the digital ID included in the notes of the photos.[24]

Between 1870 and 1920, approximately twenty million Europeans immigrated to the United States. Before 1890, most European immigrants came from nations in the western and central regions. After 1890, the influx was mainly from southern and eastern Europe. In 1892, Ellis Island was opened to accommodate the processing of the increasing number of people seeking entry to the United States.[25]

Often, the immigrants arriving between 1870 and 1920 are described as being from the lower classes, largely uneducated and poor. While many people were what poet Emma Lazarus called the "huddled masses" in her poem on the Statue of Liberty, the immigrants represented virtually all classes, including the wealthy and highly educated.

The following exercise explores the nature of primary sources by having groups of students read different photos, showing immigrants of varied classes, ages, and gender. It also involves students making inferences about the immigrant experience by writing a four-line poem modeled on the diamante often used in art education. The exercise takes one class period or less depending upon the time frame. It meets Common Core literacy anchor standards: Key Ideas 1–6, Craft and Structure 1–4, and Integration of Knowledge/Ideas 3.

Topic: European Immigrants Arriving in the United States, Early 1900s

Objectives: By the end of this exercise, students will be able to:

1. Read a photograph for content.
2. Make inferences about European immigrants based on the reading of the photograph.
3. Describe photographs as being subjective and incomplete by nature.

Procedures:

1. Introduction

   Introduce the topic of European immigrants arriving at Ellis Island. Query students about their knowledge of Ellis Island and European immigration at the turn of the twentieth century, noting almost twenty million Europeans came to the United States between 1870 and 1920. Introduce the activity of reading photographs by using the worksheet.

2. Studying Photographs

   Divide students into pairs. Distribute one photo example and worksheet (see below for worksheet questions) to half the pairs and the other photo example and worksheet to the other pairs, telling students they are to work solely in their pairs.

   Review the worksheet instructions, and have students complete the top half, answering the five questions.

   After students complete the photo reading, introduce the poem and go over the worksheet instructions. Have students write the poems.

   Have students share their poems, stressing the performance nature of the recitation. After each pair reads their poem, have students applaud the effort by snapping their fingers, the way poetry reading is typically applauded.

3. Exploring the Immigrants

   Discuss the people in the photo, asking students about how many people there are, what they are wearing, gender, age, and economic class. Stress the economic class aspect, as one photo features a woman and boy that seem to come from the upper classes. Either the students will guess they are looking at different photos or they will look puzzled over the details not in their photo.

   Identify the photos as being different, and discuss how photos are subjective since they present one point of view and incomplete in that they do not tell the whole story. Discuss issues that could arise if only one photo of the immigrants showing only one economic class was used. Would that distort history? Ask if they would like to be perceived in that way, or, better yet, not perceived at all.

4. Conclusion

    Review the exercise, briefly discussing what they learned about European immigrants from the photographs. Discuss what they did not learn.

    Close the exercise by asking students what they learned about the photos and how they would use them in their studies in the future.

European Immigrants Arriving in the United States, Early 1900s Worksheet Questions

The following questions are provided for use in a worksheet. There are two parts to the exercise as indicated below.

Reading the Photograph: What do you see?

Please answer the following questions.

1. Who is in the photo?
2. Describe these people (gender, age, dress, anything else).
3. What are they doing?
4. Where are they?
5. Using the answers to the above questions, in one word, describe the people in the photograph.

Exploring the Photo: What do you think?

On the lines below, write a four-line poem that describes the photograph as follows:

On line 1, write the one-word answer to question 5 above.

On line 2, write an action phrase that describes how these people feel.

On line 3, write an action phrase that describes what they hear and smell.

On line 4, write a one-word caption for the photograph.

WHAT TYPE OF COMMUNITY IS IT?

Developed for use in lower grades in which community is generally studied, this exercise is similar to the European immigration activity above. The traditional social studies curriculum follows the expanding environment approach. In kindergarten and first grade, the focus is on self, family, home, and school. Neighborhood is studied in second grade and larger local communities in third, such as city, suburb, and rural area. Fourth grade focuses on the state and/or regions.

Context is needed for the exercise. Depending upon the grade, the suggestion here is to have students study a range of communities, not one community, over the school year. The study should follow a pattern so that students explore geography, history, government, economy, and social aspects of each community. It also is recommended that the various communities studied be compared so students get a greater understanding of how they are similar and different. For example, in second grade, students can study a range of neighborhoods from their own to different types past and present locally, nationally, and internationally. After the first unit, every other unit would include a segment on comparing neighborhoods.

The exercise has student groups read different photographs that show diverse components of the same community. Photographs are used so that real communities are explored. They should all show the outside world. One group could read a photo that shows a retail street and stores. Other groups could have photos showing higher economic class residences, a lower economic class area, or an industrial area.

If need be, teachers can construct a worksheet for the students. A worksheet is not provided, as constructing a generic model cannot address different student reading levels. Instead, the questions below are provided as examples of the types of queries that can be used. Students read the photo to identify important content items. Next, they discuss what type of community is shown in the photo and write a caption that identifies the community type. These first two questions help students focus on the photograph and its details.

1. What is the first thing you see?
2. What is in the center of the photograph?

These two questions help students draw upon prior knowledge and experience to identify familiar and unfamiliar items.

1. Do you see anything familiar in the photo? What are those familiar things?
2. Do you see anything that is unfamiliar? What do you think these things are?

The following questions stress details.

1. Who is in the photo? Describe who they are (men, women, children), what they are wearing, and what they are doing.

2. What buildings do you see? Are there homes, stores, some other type of building? What else do you see—streets, trees, cars, anything else?
3. What else do you see?

This activity could be adapted for various grade levels.

What Type of Community Is It?

Topic: The Diversity of Communities.

Objectives: By the end of this exercise, students will be able to:

1. Read a photograph to identify characteristics of a community.
2. Write a caption describing the type of community depicted in the photographs.
3. Explain why primary sources generally, and photographs specifically, tell incomplete stories.

Procedures:

1. Introduction

   Introduce the exercise, noting that students will work in groups to read photographs, make a list of what they see, and, referring to the list, write a one-sentence caption that describes the type of community shown in the photos they read.

   Briefly model the process by projecting a photo of a different community from that to be used in the exercise. Use the questions below and, if needed, model the reading and caption writing so students are clear about what is expected of them and how to complete the exercise.

2. Exploring Community

   Divide students in groups of three and distribute a different photo to each group.

   Using the questions provided, students work in groups to read the photo, make a list of what they saw, and write the caption.

   Share the captions orally, writing each of them on the board so that every student can see them. Instruct students not to ask questions until all the captions have been presented. After all the captions have been presented, review the list and ask students what they notice. They should quickly grasp the similarities and differences between some captions, leading to the use of different photographs.

Explain that the photographs show the same community. Ask students what they would learn about that community if they only saw one photo. Discuss how photos tell only part of a story, and use examples relevant to students, such as a family picture that only shows certain members rather than everyone.

Have students review all the photos to gain a better picture of the community. Discuss why looking at more than one picture of a community provides a fuller view.

3. Conclusion

Ask students what they learned about photographs and how they would want to use them in the future.

Ask students what they learned about the community from the photos. If this is the first lesson on the community, ask what they would like to learn more about.

USING PRIMARY SOURCES TO OPEN A UNIT OF STUDY

Often, the opening of a unit sets the tone for what follows. Using inquiry-based learning to study a primary source document in the first lesson serves multiple purposes. The teacher sets the tone of the classroom by introducing the methods and a major learning resource. The opening lesson acts as a "hook" and a model.

By immediately engaging the students in primary source document study, it serves several purposes:

- sparks student interest, increasing their motivation to learn about the topic
- sets up the pattern of instruction, showing students the routine
- lets students know they will be responsible for their learning by actively engaging them in exploring texts and making decisions
- makes students aware that primary source documents will be regularly used as texts

The opening lesson also serves other important purposes. It can act as a diagnostic to evaluate the prior knowledge of students and their skills proficiency. Depending upon student competency, the lesson begins the inquiry process either by presenting the compelling question or by having the students pose the query. In addition, students begin building the database of information, and important concepts and vocabulary are introduced.

Three important planning questions for the teacher are:

1. How many primary source documents should be used?
2. What type of primary source document works best?
3. Should the lesson feature whole class, group, or individual work?

While the answers generally depend upon the situation, the multiple tasks involved in the exercise make careful time management essential.

In the examples below, the stress is on reading to access content, building a database of content information, and possibly posing questions for further study. Class time to record, share, and possibly synthesize notes is needed.

Since the activity involves close study of the source or sources, a good rule of thumb is one page for one class period. One-page documents generally provide enough time for careful study and yield enough information to make their analysis worthwhile. My preference is for visual documents since they work well in whole-class work and can easily accommodate different student needs. But it is possible to use brief print documents or excerpts. If group work is planned, a mix of types may work best.

A pivotal rule is that every student must have the same database of information. Sharing notes takes time, as does recording the notes on a master list for students to use later in the inquiry process. Group work implies that each group provides information, although there might be a significant overlap of data. Selection of primary source documents can ensure that some overlap occurs but that each primary source contributes new information.

The last task involves posing questions for further study. When the compelling question has been provided, the questions students develop are more focused, aiming at probing into aspects that will help answer that larger query. Students should only develop the compelling question when the teacher provides heavy facilitation of the process or when they have demonstrated the ability to do so from previous units.

WHAT DID ANCIENT EGYPTIAN SOCIETY
NEED TO HAVE TO BUILD THE PYRAMIDS?

This exercise has students open a unit on ancient Egypt by reading a photo of a pyramid. It also could be used to open a unit on first civilizations, with Egypt being one of the examples studied. After identifying components of the pyramid, they infer what aspects of society were needed to build the pyramid, such as population, food supply, natural resources, transportation, technology, education, architecture and engineering, and government.

Students then organize the items into categories (government, economics, social systems, and geography). The categories and the items begin the process of creating the database of information on Egypt, with the proviso that many items listed are inferences and need to be verified by further study.

Next, based on the categories and the items, students pose questions to focus their study of ancient Egypt.

Since the unit on first civilizations is early in the school year and students may be new to the inquiry method, the teacher should provide the compelling question. The activity is geared for middle and high school world history courses. It meets Common Core Reading Standards for Social Studies and History 1 and 6.

Topic: What Did Ancient Egyptian Society Need to Have to Build the Pyramids?

Objectives: By the end of this exercise, students will be able to:

1. Identify components of a pyramid.
2. Create a list of societal aspects ancient Egypt would have needed to have to build a pyramid.
3. Categorize the list of items.
4. Pose questions to focus the study of ancient Egypt.

Procedures:

1. Introduction

   Introduce ancient Egypt as the unit of study, asking students what first comes to their minds when they think of ancient Egypt. Pyramids are a likely answer.

   Project a photograph of an Egyptian pyramid, and read it as a class to identify its components—size, shape, materials used. Query students about the function of pyramids in ancient Egyptian society, writing down their ideas.

2. What Did Ancient Egypt Need to Have to Build the Pyramids?

   Ask students what ancient Egyptian society needed to have to build the pyramids, facilitating the discussion with leading questions as needed. Write the various items on the board, eliminating duplications.

   Facilitate a discussion to organize the items into categories, such as geography, government, economics, and social systems.

3. Conclusion

Using the findings of the previous exercises, facilitate a discussion that has students pose two to three supporting questions to focus their study of ancient Egypt.

"I'D RATHER NOT BE ON RELIEF"

Written by a Dust Bowl migrant in the late 1930s, this song can used to open a unit on the Great Depression/New Deal. Song lyrics are excellent print primary source documents because their language is generally accessible and their length fits within the time constraints of a single class period. Equally important, many songs provide insight into events, ideas, and emotions of the time.

Lester Hunter wrote the song. It was collected at the Shafter FSA Camp in California in 1938. "I'd Rather Not Be on Relief" offers firsthand, direct information on the feelings of Dust Bowl migrants unable to find work who needed, but as Hunter states, did not want, government relief. The song lyrics can be accessed at the "Voices from the Dust Bowl: The Charles L. Todd and Robert Sonkin Migrant Worker Collection, 1940–1941," on the Library of Congress website (www.loc.gov).

Either the entire song or selected verses can be used in the exercise. If group work is planned, each group can study a verse. Whole-class discussion can help connect the verses to gain a sense of the entire song.

The exercise can be used in any U.S. history course. It follows procedures similar to the ancient Egypt exercise in that students read the lyrics for content, compile information, make inferences about the Great Depression/New Deal based on the information, and pose a compelling question(s) for further study.

Because students should already have substantial experience with this introductory inquiry exercise, they should have the ability to create the compelling question. Given the two topics, the Great Depression and the New Deal, it is possible that two compelling questions will be needed. The exercise meets Common Core reading standards in history and social studies: Key Ideas and Details 1–5, Craft and Structure 1–4, and Integration of Knowledge and Ideas 2.

Topic: Work and Relief in the 1930s

Objectives: By the end of this exercise, students will be able to:

1. Identify the conditions many workers faced during the Great Depression.
2. Make inferences about the connection between the impact of the Great Depression and the actions taken by the federal government to address this impact.

3. Pose two compelling questions to study the Great Depression and the New Deal era.

Procedures:

1. Introduction

    Introduce the unit, noting that it has two topics: the Great Depression and the New Deal.

    Explain that students will study a primary source song lyric written by someone affected by the Great Depression and use it to craft two compelling questions for the unit, one for the Great Depression and one for the New Deal.

    Query students about what they know about the two topics, and record their answers.

2. Reading the Song Lyric

    Distribute the song lyric, and note that the composer was a victim of the Dust Bowl. Ask students what they know about the Dust Bowl, and briefly supplement their information as needed to identify what it was, when it happened, and where it happened.

    Have students in pairs read the lyrics to identify content. Share findings and record information on the board.

    In pairs, have students review the song's lyric to identify its structure, wording, rhythm, and rhyme scheme. Discuss findings, recording notes as needed, and then discuss how song lyrics uniquely express their message.

3. Crafting the Compelling Questions

    Explain that students will be organizing information into two topic categories: Great Depression and New Deal. Note that there can be overlap of information, since some data may fit in both unit categories.

    Have students in groups of four organize the information. If desired, have half the groups focus on the Great Depression and half on the New Deal.

    Share the findings and synthesize them into a single database.

    As a whole class, create the compelling questions.

4. Conclusion

    Review compelling questions and adjust as needed, noting that future adjustments may be needed.

    Introduce the next steps in the study of the unit.

WHAT DID A COMMUNITY NEED TO
BUILD AND MAINTAIN THIS STRUCTURE?

Geared for grades K–3, this exercise follows the same procedures as "What did ancient Egyptian society need to have to build the pyramids?" The primary source document should come from the community being studied.

A visual primary source is highly recommended. It is possible to take a photo of a building, a park, a school, or some other community feature and use it as the text. The questions need to be appropriate for the grade level. The title of the exercise should be adapted to identify the exact structure, park, or other item featured in the primary source.

Topic: What Did a Community Need to Have to Build and Maintain (Insert Name)

Objectives: By the end of the exercise, students will be able to:

1. Identify components of the (insert community name).
2. List characteristics of the community being studied.
3. Define important vocabulary terms.

Procedures:

1. Introduction

   Inform students they are starting a new topic of study. Identify the community. Ask students if any of them know anything about the community, and record their answers.

   Tell students they will be reading a picture to find out information about the community.

2. Reading the Picture

   Project the picture and ask students if they know what it is. Prompt them with questions if they cannot identify it.

   Ask them to look at the picture and write down what they see, or lead a discussion having students tell what they see, recording the answers. Prompt students as needed to identify important features. Have students identify a certain number of features depending upon grade level and ability, probably no more than ten.

   Review the items, and have students write their own list.

   Go over the list and provide definitions to items as needed, telling students that these items will be their vocabulary words.

3. Exploring the Community

Ask students if building the subject of the picture looked like a big job. Tell them the next step is thinking about what the community needed to build it and to keep it nice.

Lead the discussion, focusing on three categories, such as people, land, and resources. The categories can change to reflect the subject of the picture. Ask students questions, prompting them as needed. Record the answers, and, as above, identify vocabulary words.

4. Conclusion

Review the lesson, the list, and the vocabulary words.
Introduce the next lesson.

DOCUMENT-BASED QUESTIONS (DBQ)

The Document-Based Question (DBQ) has become increasingly popular in recent years for a couple of reasons. A major factor is the inclusion of DBQs on Advanced Placement and other exams.[26] Another influence has been the rise in the use of primary source documents as learning texts. With the stress in Common Core literacy standards on progressive use of texts, both trends are likely to intensify.

There are two types of DBQs. Both types require students to answer questions by writing an essay that has a thesis and is supported by evidence that is presented as part of a well-reasoned argument.

The exam DBQ has students answer an essay question, using information from a selection of documents to answer the essay question. The time limitations of the exam determine the number (generally eight to ten) and, to a certain extent, the type of documents as well as their length. Written documents need to be brief and to the point. They tend to be excerpts of a larger document.

The other DBQ is an inquiry method that uses documents throughout the study of a topic, often has complete written documents or longer excerpts, and may have students pose and then answer questions. The DBQ process frames the learning. The big-picture model discussed above is a document-based question-inquiry method. The discussion here focuses on the DBQ assessment.

To successfully complete a DBQ exam question, students must possess substantial content understanding and mastery of diverse skills. The DBQ is a culmination, a summative assessment. It works best when students have proceeded through a larger inquiry process that has them literally climb Bloom's taxonomy from the lowest to the highest levels. The success of the DBQ assessment depends upon student familiarity with the DBQ method, their understanding of pertinent historical content, and their proficiency in reading, thinking, and writing.

As a result, in preparation for the DBQ exam, teachers need to design a clear, strategic sequence of progressive learning that integrates building understanding of content with the development of skills. Since the documents supply the texts students use to improve their competency, their selection requires great care and consideration. Most important is ensuring the documents are at the appropriate reading level of students.

Given the stress on student progress, in a sense, choosing the documents organizes the learning over time. If all of the above requirements are met, the DBQ exam can effectively evaluate student learning. Another point is that DBQs meet virtually every Common Core reading standard for history and social studies.

Elements of an Effective Document-Based Question

Designing and developing a DBQ assessment requires the teacher to carefully consider exactly what the purpose of the inquiry is regarding student achievement, why the DBQ is being used, and how it fits within the larger context of learning. In some cases, the DBQ inquiry method is the larger learning context, with the assessment acting as its conclusion.

Because the DBQ exam has a restricted time frame, posing the question and the careful selection of documents are important tasks that ensure the success of the assessment.

As is true for inquiry generally, but is even more important for the DBQ assessment, the question is the pivot around which the exercise revolves. Brief and concisely stated in jargon-free and grade-appropriate language, it should include information about the people, place, and time context as well as relevant subtopics or themes. The question is open ended. Fewer words are better.

The assessment question has the same three components as any compelling question. Though discussed above, it bears revisiting here in more detail. When the compelling question of the larger inquiry process is the query for the DBQ, students will already be familiar with its wording and intent. What follows is for situations in which the question is different.

In a time-constrained DBQ, clarity is essential. Students have a finite amount of time to complete the exercise. An unclear question could eat up much of that time. The wording of the question should clearly identify the topic and the task as well as provide examples.

The topic addresses an important aspect of the period. It can be the unit topic or a pertinent subtopic. It should be of interest to students and draw upon their prior knowledge.

What Students Need to Know and Be Able to Do to Complete a DBQ Inquiry Successfully

Knowledge		Ability

Content

Knowledge:
- Understand period's history (people, places, and events); important subtopics; and themes.
- Connect DBQ topic and questions to period's history.

Ability:
- Apply understanding of period to document.
- Select content, organize it for analysis.
- Develop thesis, arguments, and evidence to support thesis.
- Write well-reasoned, coherent essay to support thesis

Document

Knowledge:
- What primary and secondary sources are: differences, subjective, incomplete nature of primary sources; nature/qualities of specific types of sources.

Ability:
- Read document for content.
- Assess document for validity, bias, accuracy.
- Compare/evaluate content from multiple documents.

Question

Knowledge:
- Question's meaning: interrogatives, verbs; people, place, and time parameters.
- How/why question relates to period/topic.

Ability:
- Read question to : identify topic, define task, identify examples to use to complete DBQ.

Figure 2.2.
Author created

Interrogatives and possibly specific action verbs identify the task. Students should know the meaning of the verb and understand what it is asking them to do. For example, *analyze* is often used but is vague, open to varying interpretations. Conversely, focusing on verbs such as *explain* or *evaluate* helps specify the task. *Explain* indicates that students will answer the question why. *Evaluate* implies that they will be making a judgment call on the efficacy, significance, or some other aspect of the topic. The examples to be used to answer the question are often included in the query. The information in the examples helps students better understand the question.

For example, "Why are the economic times of the 1930s called the Great Depression?" assesses a unit on the Great Depression/New Deal. The topic is the economic times of the 1930s. The task is to answer why it is considered the Great Depression. The example is the severity of the 1930s depression that earned its *great* title. Depending upon document selection, the question implies comparing the hard times of the 1930s to other similar periods in the past. Though simply phrased, this question asks students to apply their prior knowledge of past hard times to assess severity.

The second criterion of DBQ assessment success is careful, strategic selection and possibly editing of the primary and secondary source documents students will use to answer the question. A diverse set of documents of varying types is basic to the DBQ. Readability is pivotal. If the students can't read the documents, the entire process falters.

Length is another issue. Typically, one-to-two-paragraph print excerpts work best. So students can adequately analyze the documents, the thrust and bias must be retained. Another consideration is providing documents with differing points of view so students can exercise high-level thinking skills.

An important resource is the textbook. The textbook narrative is a secondary source and can be excerpted as needed. Textbooks also contain a wealth of primary sources of various types. Many also come with ancillary volumes or CD-ROMs of primary sources. High school textbooks for Advanced Placement (AP) classes are particularly well suited for DBQ use, as the DBQ is part of the AP exam. Numerous primary source readers also are available.

Recommending specific documents is difficult because they need to be fitted to individual classroom needs, and some teachers may have difficulty accessing certain documents. However, it is possible to make some general recommendations from the exercise examples above to provide greater insight into the types of sources available.

For the Great Depression DBQ, the song lyric used in the example on opening a unit is a good choice. Photographs of the impact of the Depression are readily available on the Library of Congress website as well as in textbooks. Editorial cartoons also are available in textbooks. Transcripts of speeches, including the 1934 inaugural address by President Franklin D. Roo-sevelt, are excellent documents. Letters and interviews from those affected by the hard times are usually included in primary source readers. If comparison to previous hard times is desired, then similar documents from the recession of the early 1870s or 1890s can be used.

By amassing an array of diverse documents that provide varying perspec-tives, the documents offer a rich, robust body of information for students to use in answering the DBQ on why the hard times of the 1930s are called the Great Depression.

USING VISUALS TO MEET THE NEEDS OF ALL STUDENTS

Recent trends in the student population and advances in scholarship have made every educational professional more aware that teaching and learning must ac-commodate English-language learners (ELL) and students with special needs.

Over the last few decades, our population has become more diverse, more multicultural, and more multilingual. It is rare to find a school where only one language is spoken.

Similarly, our knowledge of the brain and of a large array of special needs as well as changes in public policy have helped transform our educational system to better accommodate all student learners. Universal Design for Learning (UDL) is a set of principles used to guide curriculum development so that all students have an opportunity to learn.[27]

The implications of an all-learner curriculum are that it will accommodate each and every student. In practice, the curriculum helps all students learn to the best of their ability whether or not they have a special need.

For our purposes, research and classroom experience has shown that us-ing visual primary sources and visual graphic organizers can help English-language learners and many students with special needs learn at a higher level.[28] Print poses issues of decoding as well as vocabulary and language, among other things not present with visuals. Pictorial primary sources ap-parently speak a universal language more easily deciphered by all students. Graphic organizers provide a visual learning aid that can be used effectively by English-language learners and various special-needs students.

Another strategy that works for all learners is differentiation. This short description cannot provide a full account of differentiation. Suffice it to say that it generally involves the teacher and students forming a strong classroom community based on mutual respect. The teacher designs learning exercises geared to the differing ways students learn so that all can contribute to the learning process.[29]

As has been noted likely too often, an important consideration is structuring learning around a carefully crafted sequential, progressive curriculum that has well-defined levels and steps within those levels so that students can perform according to their ability. The progression facilitates student improvement.

Primary sources can support the education of all learners by providing students with learning resources tailored to their strengths and needs but also working to improve areas of weakness. For example, teachers might stress the use of visual primary sources with ELL students but include instruction aimed to improve their ability to read English-language printed text and writing.

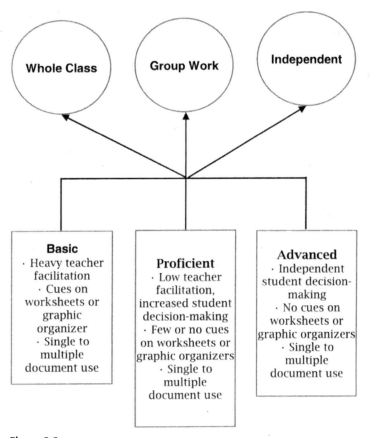

Developing a Sequential, Progressive Curriculum for All Learners

Figure 2.3.
Author created

NOTES

1. Keith C. Barton, "Primary Sources in History: Breaking through the Myths," *Phi Delta Kappan*, 86 (2005): 745–53, examines myths surrounding the use of primary sources but also points out their value. See also David Eicher, "Primary Sources: Handle with Care, But DO Handle," *Writer*, 120 (2007): 34–37.

2. Brett Levy et al., "Examining Studies of Inquiry-Based Learning in Three Fields of Education: Sparking Generative Conversation," *Journal of Teacher Education*, 64 (2013): 389.

3. Joseph J. Gonzalez, "My Journey with Inquiry-Based Learning," *Journal on Excellence in College Teaching*, 24 (2013): 37; Eva Marie Kane, "Urban Student Motivation through Inquiry-Based Learning," *Journal of Studies in Education*, 3 (2013): 163–5.

4. Kirk Ankeney, Richard Del Rio, Gary B. Nash, David Vigilante (eds.), *Bring History Alive: A Sourcebook for Teaching United States History* (Los Angeles: National Center for History in the Schools, UCLA, 1996), iii; Sam Wineburg, *Historical Thinking and Other Unnatural Acts* (Philadelphia: Temple University Press, 2001).

5. Keith Barton and Linda Levstik, "Why Don't More History Teachers Engage Students in Interpretation?" *Social Education*, 6 (2003): 358–9.

6. Levy et al., "Examining Studies of Inquiry-Based Learning in Three Fields of Education: Sparking Generative Conversation," 394.

7. Barton and Levstik, "Why Don't More History Teachers Engage Students in Interpretation?" 359.

8. In describing his experience with IBL, Gonzalez offers excellent examples and solutions to various issues that can arise when teaching and learning turns to inquiry. He stresses scaffolding and group work as well as a heavy dose of teacher research. Gonzalez, "My Journey with Inquiry-Based Learning," 37–45.

9. Kane, "Urban Student Motivation through Inquiry-Based Learning," 167.

10. Mark Newman, "The 'Big Picture' Model for Learning World History, or Slipping Between the Rocks and Hard Places," *Teaching History: A Journal of Methods*, 29 (2004): 59–70.

11. National Council for the Social Studies (NCSS), *College, Career, & Civic Life (C3) Framework for Social Studies State Standards: Guidance for Enhancing the Rigor of K–12 Civics, Economics, Geography, and History* (Silver Spring, MD: NCSS, 2013), 12, 16–20.

12. James Blaut et al., "Mapping as a Cultural and Cognitive Universal," *Annals of the Association of American Geographers*, 93 (2003): 165–85.

13. Jerry Brotton, *A History of the World in 12 Maps* (New York: Viking, 2012), 10–11, 57–58, 139–40; B. L. Gordon, "Sacred Directions, Orientation, and the Top of the Map," *History of Religions*, 10 (1971): 211–27.

14. Gordon, "Sacred Directions, Orientation, and the Top of the Map," 223.

15. World Map by Ptolemy, Library of Congress Rare Books and Special Collections Division, Washington, DC, http://hdl.loc.gov/loc.pnp/cph.3c10342.

16. Al-Idrisi Map of the world, http://commons.wikimedia.org/wiki/File:Al -Idrisi%27s_world_map.JPG.

17. The Hereford map redrawing can be viewed at http://cartographic-images.net/ Cartographic_Images/226_The_Hereford_Mappamundi.html.

18. Brotton, *A History of the World in 12 Maps*, 72, 85.

19. Ibid., 19; Robin Lane Fox, *The Classical World: An Epic History from Homer to Hadrian* (New York: Basic Books, 2006), 250–4.

20. Brotton, *A History of the World in 12 Maps*, 82–113.

21. Ibid., 54–81.

22. Ibid., 82–113. See also Peter Brown, *The Rise of Western Christendom: Triumph and Diversity, AD 200–1000*, second edition (Oxford, England: Wiley-Blackwell, 2007), and Richard Fletcher, *The Barbarian Conversion: From Paganism to Christianity* (Berkeley: University of California Press, 1997).

23. A brief description of the formation of the committee and the writing of the document is in Walter Isaacson, *Benjamin Franklin: An American Life* (New York: Simon and Schuster, 2003), 307–13.

24. *Immigrants Carrying Luggage, Ellis Island, New York*. Library of Congress Prints and Photographs Division, Library of Congress, Washington, DC, http://hdl.loc .gov/loc.pnp/ggbain.03252; *Ellis Island*, Library of Congress Prints and Photographs Division, Library of Congress, Washington, DC, http://hdl.loc.gov/loc.pnp/ggbain.50438.

25. U.S. Bureau of the Census, *Historical Statistics of the United States, 1789–1945* (Washington, DC: U. S. Government Printing Office, 1949), 33–34.

26. Eric Rothschild, "The Impact of the Document-Based Question on the Teaching of United States History," *The History Teacher*, 33 (2000): 485–500; Timothy Hacsi, "Document-Based Question: What Is the Historical Significance of the Advanced Placement Test?" *Journal of American History*, 90 (2004): 1392–1400.

27. A good resource for Universal Design for Learning is the National Center on Universal Design for Learning at www.udlcenter.org.

28. Cynthia Salinas, Maria Franquiz, and Steve Guberman, "Introducing Historical Thinking to Second Language Learners: What Students Know and What They Want to Know," *The Social Studies*, 97 (2006): 205.

29. Carol Ann Tomlinson has written extensively on differentiation. Her initial volume is *The Differentiated Classroom: Responding to the Needs of All Learners* (Alexandria, VA: ASCD, 1999).

Part Three

Accommodating Common Core

While there has been much ado about the Common Core movement, there also has been much confusion. The discussion here does not defend or criticize Common Core. Instead, it seeks to explain the standards and to provide some ideas on accommodating them. For history and social studies, two standards efforts are pertinent. First, the Common Core Literacy Standards focus on grades six through twelve. General Common Core Reading standards apply to earlier grades instruction in the content area. Second, the C3 Framework for State Social Studies Standards identifies core content areas (civics, economics, geography, and history), provides an inquiry arc as the method of teaching and learning, and offers standards in the core content areas.

ACCOMMODATING COMMON CORE LITERACY STANDARDS

The place to start is with the Common Core literacy standards booklet, as it provides some clarity. Perhaps the best way to begin is by identifying what the Common Core literacy standards are and what they are not. An important point is that the C3 Framework for State Social Studies Standards requires integration of the literacy standards.

Simply put, Common Core literacy standards aim to ensure that all students are college and career ready in literacy by the end of high school. The standards also provide an idea of what the authors think it means to be literate in the twenty-first century. That idea deserves full attention since it offers insight into expectations and the ultimate goal of educating young people to be responsible citizens. What does it mean for a student to meet the Common Core literacy standards? The booklet states:

Students who meet the Standards readily undertake the close, attentive reading that is at the heart of understanding and enjoying complex works of literature. They habitually perform the critical reading necessary to pick carefully through the staggering amount of information available today in print and digitally. They actively seek the wide, deep, and thoughtful engagement with high-quality literary and informational texts that builds knowledge, enlarges experience, and broadens worldviews. They reflexively demonstrate the cogent reasoning and use of evidence that is essential to both private deliberation and responsible citizenship in a democratic republic.[1]

The implication is that students who are college and career ready are independent learners. They possess strong content knowledge. They adapt their communication to their audience, their task, their purpose, and their discipline. They are engaged, knowing how to comprehend and how to critique. They use pertinent evidence to support their findings. They recognize the strengths and the limitations of technology, using it to good purpose. They understand other perspectives and cultures.[2]

Regarding specific skills, the Common Core literacy standards stress reading, writing, speaking, and listening. Implied in all these areas is critical thinking. Another important point is that the Common Core literacy standards focus on results, on outcomes. Lastly, in history and social studies, the use of varied types of primary sources is mandated at all levels.

The discussion here focuses on the history/social studies reading standards. They are divided into three categories—key ideas and details, craft and structure, and integration of knowledge and ideas. They are organized into anchor standards that are general statements and grade-level specific standards (six to eight, nine to ten, and eleven to twelve) that provide more detailed application of the anchors.

Each competency level aims at independent proficiency. Across grades, the standards follow a progressive sequence of difficulty. For example, standard 1 in grades six to eight has students "cite specific textual evidence to support analysis of primary and secondary sources."

In grades nine to ten, students cite textual evidence, but the standards add the specific focus on "date and origin of the information."

Grades eleven through twelve take the standard one step further, asking students to connect "insights gained from specific details to an understanding of the text as a whole."

Equally important, the last standard for each grade-level sequence has the same goal, with one major distinction—the complexity of the texts increases across the grade levels. The reading standard 10 requires students to read and comprehend independently and proficiently.[3]

Since the Common Core standards require increased competency at the end of two-year grade-level cycles, they require long-term planning so that students can learn progressively at higher levels of competency. Because the grade-level specific standards are basically subsets of the anchors, teachers can use the fourteen anchor standards to develop a progressive, sequential, spiral literacy curriculum that is easily adapted to their grade and that meets the needs of their students.

Before examining the spiral curriculum idea, perhaps it would be helpful to identify what the Common Core standards are not. At the most general level, the standards do not "define the whole of college and career readiness."

In terms of specifics, first and foremost, the standards do not mandate how teachers should teach, nor do they identify everything students should know and be able to do. While the standards provide outcomes, they do not define the entire curriculum. The standards do not "enumerate all or even most of the content that students should learn." Nor do they identify "all that can or should be taught."

They do not define what intervention methods and materials to use for underperforming or excelling students. They do not identify "the full range of supports appropriate for English language learners and for students with special needs."[4]

To sum up, the Common Core Literacy Standards for History/Social Studies identify a range of fundamental literacy skills in which all students should have a common proficiency. They are not the be-all and end-all of history/social studies education. But they do mandate a heavy integration of primary sources into teaching and learning.

Vital Witnesses provides strategies and ideas for the effective use of primary sources in the classroom. The Common Core Literacy Standards add another layer that needs some explanation. Two suggestions are discussed here.

The first deals with the need for long-term planning that the big-picture inquiry model requires and is mandated by Common Core competency levels. What is described here can easily be absorbed into the big picture or any other inquiry model. It adapts the spiral curriculum strategy common in math to history and social studies courses. The spiral curriculum supplies a progressive, sequential way for students to practice skills and build content mastery over time. It involves revisiting content and skills previously learned as enrichment and then proceeding to a higher level of learning.

The progressive learning sequence follows the same path as the one described in the discussion on the big-picture model. Learning moves from whole class to group to independent based on proficiency. Teacher presence recedes over time and student independence increases, also based on proficiency. Similarly, primary source use moves from a single text of one type to multiple texts either of one type or mixed types.

Much of what is described here is familiar territory. The course acts as the blank canvas, so to speak, of teaching and learning. Unit topics break up the course into manageable teaching and learning constructs. Themes extending across the course connect the flow of teaching and learning across the units. The Common Core literacy standards would be one theme.

The suggestion here is to use the week or some other smaller time span as a subset of the unit topic, establishing a learning routine over that span that is replicated in the study of the unit topic and, by extension, the course. The rationale is to provide ample opportunity for students to practice skills and to work with content within a well-established routine.

As the course progresses and students become more familiar with the method, with the content, and with the skills, the regimen helps them improve their competency. As improvement occurs, the difficulty and independent learning increases. By maintaining the same basic pattern of learning, students can focus on improving mastery rather than having to learn a new routine while building content knowledge and skills. The chart below illustrates the spiral curriculum model.

Building a Spiral Curriculum

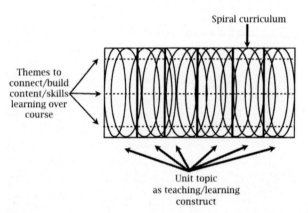

Figure 3.1.
Author created

The second suggestion is to use the anchor standards to develop the literacy curriculum, adapting the anchors to meet grade level and student needs.[5] The ultimate goal is for students to read and comprehend complex literary texts independently and proficiently. Complexity must be defined by grade level and student ability.

While the standards are divided into three categories, these divisions are not helpful in devising the curriculum. Instead, using the anchor standards as a single entity allows them to provide excellent guides. Organize the literacy curriculum into three progressive skills categories using anchor standards to define the levels. Next, list those standards most pertinent to meet that specific skill level. The two charts below show the anchor standards by category and the reconfiguration to construct the literacy curriculum.

Approaching Common Core:
THE PROGRESSIVE SEQUENCE OF LEARNING BY ANCHOR STANDARDS

Key Ideas and Details	Craft and Structure	Integration of Knowledge/Ideas
1. Read closely to determine what text says explicitly. 2. Make logical inferences. 3. Make conclusions supported with evidence. 4. Determine central ideas/themes of a text. 5. Analyze development of ideas/themes. 6. Summarize key supporting details. 7. Analyze how and why of interaction over course of a text.	1. Interpret use of words/phrases in a text. 2. Analyze how specific words shape meaning/tone. 3. Analyze structure of text including how sentence, paragraphs, etc. relate to each other. 4. Assess how point of view/purpose shape content/style of a text.	1. Integrate and evaluate content presented in diverse formats/media. 2. Delineate/evaluate argument/specific claims in a text, including validity of reasoning, relevance/sufficiency of evidence. 3. Analyze how two or more texts address similar themes to build knowledge or compare author approaches.

Read and comprehend complex literary and informational texts independently and proficiently.

Figure 3.2.
Author created

How Common Core Informs the Progressive, Sequential Curriculum

Level 1: Read closely to determine what text says explicitly	Level 2: Make logical inferences	Level 3: Analyze how two or more texts address similar themes to build knowledge or compare author approaches
• Determine central ideas/themes of a text. • Interpret use of words/phrases in a text. • Analyze how specific words shape meaning/tone. • Analyze structure of text including how sentence, paragraphs, etc. relate to each other. • Make conclusions supported by evidence. • Summarize key supporting details.	All in column to the left. • Analyze development of ideas/themes. • Analyze how and why of interaction over course of a text. • Analyze how point of view/purpose shape content/style of a text. • Delineate/evaluate argument/specific claims in a text, including validity of reasoning, relevance/sufficiency of evidence.	All in column to the immediate left. • Integrate and evaluate content presented in diverse formats/media.

Figure 3.3.
Author created

The construction of the curriculum may need some brief explanation. The use of three levels supplies milestones of proficiency and divides the curriculum into basic, intermediate, and proficient degrees of competency. Bloom's revised taxonomy informs the selection of the anchor standards to use as levels and for the listing of specific anchor standards under each level.

Note that the first two standards under "Key Ideas and Details" serve as the basic and intermediate levels. The last standard under "Integration of Knowledge/Ideas" is a natural choice for proficiency because it is the only standard that explicitly requires study of more than one text.

While other configurations of the standards are possible, the viability of the curriculum depends upon certain characteristics. The curriculum needs to:

- provide a sequential progression that allows student proficiency to be clearly evaluated over time
- institute a pattern of teaching and learning based on ongoing, regular practice that helps students build content mastery and skills competency
- maintain the long-term perspective of achieving its goal by the end of the grade level or school year

ACCOMMODATING THE C3 FRAMEWORK

The C3 Framework for State Social Studies Standards follows a similar approach to the Common Core Standards. It focuses primarily on skills. The rationale behind the C3 Framework is that students need to be able to identify problems in society, to inquire into those problems by asking questions that focus their investigations, and to develop potential solutions that lead to constructive actions. It aims at educating competent, informed, and active citizens.

Besides identifying four core content areas, content is left to the states. Unlike the Common Core, the C3 does provide a method of teaching and learning that likely will either inform or mandate how teachers teach. The Inquiry Arc is the centerpiece of the C3 Framework.[6]

Perhaps the most important point about the C3 Framework is that its audience is the state educational agency. The various classroom exercises in *Vital Witnesses* do not have C3 standards because, as the C3 Framework booklet states, "The Framework aims to support states in creating standards that prepare young people for effective and successful participation in college, careers, and civic life." It provides "states with voluntary guidance for upgrading existing social studies standards."[7] Unless otherwise stated, all quotes and references are to the C3 Framework booklet.

The process of adapting to the C3 Framework is ongoing as this book is being written. The work on social studies standards revision has not been completed. As was the case with Common Core, C3 includes a disclaimer as to what it is not attempting to do. It does not encompass everything that might be included in social studies standards, nor does it mandate what content should be taught at the varying grade levels, leaving those decisions to the states. However, it does include over three hundred standards, making the Framework an unwieldy guide.

What does the C3 Framework attempt to do? Regarding content, it narrows the traditional social studies focus to the four core subject areas: civics, economics, geography, and history. The inclusion of civics and geography are long overdue and can help upgrade teaching and learning in these areas. But it downgrades the remaining social sciences and psychology to secondary status.

The Framework focuses on "key concepts and skills students should develop through a robust social studies program."[8] These concepts and skills are organized by the core discipline—civics, economics, geography, and history.

The Inquiry Arc ties everything together, supplying the method that students use to learn social studies. It is organized around compelling questions that identify a topic of study and supporting questions that help students inquire into the compelling question. As students proceed through the inquiry process, they apply disciplinary tools and concepts. They evaluate sources to identify pertinent evidence. Lastly, they develop conclusions and present their findings, possibly taking informed action.

Depending upon state adoption or adaptation of the C3 Framework, it does mandate that teachers follow an inquiry method of teaching and learning. *Vital Witnesses* recommends inquiry, too.

Accommodating the C3 Framework involves a similar strategy to that presented for the literacy standards. Basically, it requires long-term planning to build a progressive, sequential learning curriculum. In fact, the suggestion is to use the literacy spiral curriculum and the big picture or some other inquiry model to accommodate the C3 Framework. The four core content areas and the social sciences can act as content themes.

The chart below depicts the spiral curriculum as it applies to the academic course and the unit. In the C3 context, the spiral curriculum is structured around the Inquiry Arc to facilitate the progressive learning sequence for mastery of the inquiry process, content knowledge, and disciplinary skills over time. The progressive learning sequence is based on improved student competency, leading to reduced teacher presence and increased student independence and responsibility over time.

Accommodating the C3 Framework by Building a Progressive, Sequential Learning Curriculum

Course Subject

Discipline as Themes	Unit Topic	Unit Topic	Unit Topic	Unit Topic	Unit Topic
Civics					
Economics					
Geography		Questions Data Sources Key Concepts Key Strategies			
History					
Social Systems					

—— **Inquiry Arc Spiral Curriculum** ——

Unit of Study

Disciplines as Themes	Dimension 1 Questions	Dimension 2 Data Sources	Dimension 3 Key Concepts	Dimension 4 Key Strategies
Civics				
Economics				
Geography		Unit topic related to big picture content. Disciplines serve as themes across units, acting as connectors. One discipline may dominate but others also are studied in relation to that dominant discipline.		
History				
Social Systems				

Figure 3.4.
Author created

NOTES

1. Common Core State Standards Initiative, *Common Core Standards for English Language Arts & Literacy in History/Social Studies, Science, and Technical Subjects* (2010), www.corestandards.org/ELA-Literacy, 3, accessed January 30, 2014.

2. Ibid., 7.

3. Ibid., 61.

4. Ibid., 6.

5. Ibid., 60.

6. National Council for the Social Studies (NCSS), *College, Career, and Civic Life (C3) Framework for Social Studies State Standards: Guidance for Enhancing the Rigor of K–12 Civics, Economics, Geography, and History* (Silver Spring, MD: NCSS, 2013), 12, 16–19.

7. Ibid., 6.

8. Ibid., 14.

Bibliography

BOOKS

Ankeney, Kirk, Richard Del Rio, Gary B. Nash, David Vigilante (eds.). *Bring History Alive: A Sourcebook for Teaching United States History.* Los Angeles: National Center for History in the Schools, UCLA, 1996.

Brotton, Jerry. *A History of the World in 12 Maps.* New York: Viking, 2012.

Brown, Peter. *The Rise of Western Christendom: Triumph and Diversity, AD 200–1000*, second edition. Oxford, England: Wiley-Blackwell, 2007.

Buisseret, David. *From Sea Charts to Satellite Images: Interpreting North American History through Maps.* Chicago: University of Chicago Press, 1990.

Burian, Peter, and Robert Caputo. *National Geographic Photography Field Guide.* Washington, DC: National Geographic, 2001.

Burke, Peter. *Eyewitnessing: The Uses of Images as Historical Evidence.* Ithaca, NY: Cornell University Press, 2001.

Crosby, Alfred. *Ecological Imperialism: The Biological Expansion of Europe, 900–1900.* New York: Cambridge University Press, 1986.

Cunliffe, Barry. *Europe between the Oceans, 9000 BC–AD 1000.* New Haven, CT: Yale University Press, 2008.

Danzer, Gerald. *World History: An Atlas and Study Guide.* Upper Saddle River, NJ: Prentice Hall, 1998.

Danzer, Gerald, and Mark Newman. *Tuning In: Primary Sources in the Teaching of History.* Chicago: The World History Project, The University of Illinois at Chicago, 1991.

Diamond, Jared. *Guns, Germs, and Steel: The Fates of Human Societies.* New York: W. W. Norton & Company, 1998.

Erdoes, Richard, and Alfonso Ortiz (comp. and eds.). *American Indian Myths and Legends.* New York: Pantheon, 1985.

Evans, David. *Big Road Blues: Tradition and Creativity in the Folk Blues.* Berkeley: University of California Press, 1982.

Fairbank, John K., Edwin O. Reischauer, and Albert M. Craig. *East Asia: Tradition and Transformation*, revised edition. Cambridge: Harvard University Press, 1989.

Fletcher, Richard. *The Barbarian Conversion: From Paganism to Christianity.* Berkeley: University of California Press, 1997.

Fox, Robin Lane. *The Classical World: An Epic History from Homer to Hadrian.* New York: Basic Books, 2006.

Isaacson, Walter. *Benjamin Franklin: An American Life.* New York: Simon and Schuster, 2003.

Lord, Albert. *The Singer of Tales.* Cambridge: Harvard University Press, 1981.

Mithen, Steven. *After the Ice: A Global Human History, 20,000–5,000 BC.* Cambridge: Harvard University Press, 2003.

National Council for the Social Studies (NCSS). *College, Career, and Civic Life (C3) Framework for Social Studies State Standards: Guidance for Enhancing the Rigor of K–12 Civics, Economics, Geography, and History.* Silver Spring, MD: NCSS, 2013.

Robinson, David. *From Peep Show to Palace.* New York: Columbia University Press, 1997.

Tierno, Michael. *Aristotle's Poetics for Screenwriters: Storytelling Secrets from the Greatest Mind in Western Civilization.* New York: Hyperion, 2002.

Tomlinson, Carol Ann. *The Differentiated Classroom: Responding to the Needs of All Learners.* Alexandria, VA: ASCD, 1999.

Trachtenberg, Alan (ed.). *Classic Essays on Photography.* New Haven, CT: Leete's Island Books, 1980.

U.S. Bureau of the Census. *Historical Statistics of the United States, 1789–1945.* Washington, DC: U.S. Government Printing Office, 1949.

Weslager, C. A. *The Log Cabin in America: From Pioneer Days to the Present.* New Brunswick, NJ: Rutgers University Press, 1969.

Wineburg, Sam. *Historical Thinking and Other Unnatural Acts.* Philadelphia: Temple University Press, 2001.

JOURNAL ARTICLES

Barton, Keith C. "Primary Sources in History: Breaking through the Myths," *Phi Delta Kappan*, 86 (2005): 745–53.

Barton, Keith, and Linda Levstik. "Why Don't More History Teachers Engage Students in Interpretation?" *Social Education*, 6 (2003): 358–9.

Bascom, William. "Four Functions of Folklore," *Journal of American Folklore*, 67 (1954): 333–49.

Blaut, James, David Stea, Christopher Spencer, and Mark Blades. "Mapping as a Cultural and Cognitive Universal," *Annals of the Association of American Geographers*, 93 (2003): 165–85.

Blench, Roger. "African Agricultural Tools, Implications of Synchronic Ethnography for Agrarian History" (paper presented, fifth International Workshop for African Archaeology, July 1–4, 2006, revised 2007). Accessed January 27, 2014 at Academia.edu, http://www.academia.edu/2326505/African_agricultural_tools_implications_of_synchronic_ethnography_for_agrarian_history.

Cruz, Barbara, and Stephen Thornton. "Visualizing Social Studies Literacy: Teaching Content and Skills to English Language Learners," *Social Studies Research & Practice*, 7 (2012).

Eicher, David. "Primary Sources: Handle with Care, But DO Handle," *Writer*, 120 (2007): 34–37.

Foster, George. "What Is Folk Culture?" *American Anthropologist*, 55 (1953): 159–73.

Gonzalez, Joseph J. "My Journey with Inquiry-Based Learning," *Journal on Excellence in College Teaching*, 24 (2013): 33–50.

Gordon, B. L. "Sacred Directions, Orientation, and the Top of the Map," *History of Religions*, 10 (1971): 211–27.

Hacsi, Timothy. "Document-Based Question: What Is the Significance of the Advanced Placement Test?" *Journal of American History*, 90 (2004): 1392–1400.

Husch, Gail. "George Caleb Bingham's *The Country Election*: Whig Tribute to the Will of the People," *American Art Journal*, 19 (1987): 4–22.

Kane, Eva Marie. "Urban Student Motivation through Inquiry-Based Learning," *Journal of Studies in Education*, 3 (2013): 155–68. doi: 10.5296/jse.v3il.3076.

Levy, Brett, Ebony Thomas, Kathryn Drago, and Lesley Rex. "Examining Studies of Inquiry-Based Learning in Three Fields of Education: Sparking Generative Conversation," *Journal of Teacher Education*, 64 (2013): 387–408.

McCarthy, Michael. "Political Cartoons in the History Classroom," *The History Teacher*, 11 (1977): 32–34.

Newman, Mark. "The 'Big Picture' Model for Learning World History, or Slipping Between the Rocks and Hard Places," *Teaching History: A Journal of Methods*, 29 (2004).

———. "What Do You See? Exploring the Nature of Photographs as Educational Resources," *Teaching and Learning with Primary Sources*, 1 (2009), accessed January 26, 2014, http://tpsfed.org/TPSJ.htm.

Rothschild, Eric. "The Impact of the Document-Based Question on the Teaching of United States History," *The History Teacher*, 33 (2000): 485–500.

Salinas, Cynthia, Maria Franquiz, and Steve Guberman. "Introducing Historical Thinking to Second Language Learners: Exploring What Students Know and What They Want to Know," *The Social Studies* (2006): 205.

Thomas, Samuel. "Teaching America's GAPE (or any other period) with Political Cartoons: A Systematic Approach to Primary Source Analysis," *The History Teacher*, 37 (2004): 426–7.

Woelders, Adam. "Using Film to Conduct Historical Inquiry with Middle School Students," *The History Teacher*, 40 (2007): 336–70.

Yankah, Kwesi. "Proverb Rhetoric and African Judicial Processes: The Untold Story," *Journal of American Folklore*, 99 (1986): 280–303.

WEBSITES

Cartographic images, http://cartographic-images.net.

Common Core State Standards Initiative, http://www.corestandards.org.

The Henry Ford, http://www.thehenryford.org.

Library of Congress, http://www.loc.gov.

National Center on Universal Design for Learning, http://www.udlcenter.org.

Wikimedia Commons, http://commons.wikimedia.org.